More Praise for *In the Grip of His Mercy*

"No matter how swift the transitions of the twenty-first century or dramatic the achievements by innovators, the human system must still respond and react to a multiplicity of daily pressures. *In the Grip of His Mercy* is an excellent insightful tool to be shared in a study group, Bible study, book club, church fellowship or with just a few good friends."

Bishop Vashti M. McKenzie
African Methodist Episcopal Church
Eighteenth Episcopal District
Presiding Prelate

"Bishop Hilliard has written a prescription to relieve the pain, pressure and perplexities that face every generation throughout this nation. This inspirational over-the-counter aspirin is an assault to the enemy and should be dispensed in every school, family and ministry. I am convinced that one dosage of this prescriptive formula will leave the reader Empowered for life!"

Jamal Harrison-Bryant
Empowerment Temple AME
Baltimore, MD

"*In the Grip of His Mercy* is a much-needed book for persons coping with the challenges of life while striving to live to their greatest potential. Bishop Hilliard addresses a number of barriers that many people struggle with emotionally and spiritually when confronting feelings of powerlessness and low self-esteem. With scriptural reference and the insightful experiences of a pastor, the author explains in clear language how to successfully move through painful experiences toward victorious living."

Dr. Thema Bryant-Davis
SHARE Program Coordinator
Prince⁀⁀⁀ ⁀⁀⁀⁀⁀⁀⁀⁀⁀⁀⁀ ⁀⁀⁀⁀⁀ ⁀⁀⁀ices

"Bishop Hilliard has done it again with another poignant book that raises questions, provides answers and gives the reader hope in our Lord and Savior Jesus Christ."

Dr. Jawanza Kunjufu
Author and Preacher

"Dr. Hilliard presents an extraordinarily creative book on how to live a successful life in spite of the pressures that come to all of us. He has an excellent writing style and a timely topic. *In the Grip of His Mercy* charts the course of moving us from trauma to triumph. Dr. Hilliard challenges us to grow and gives practical Bible-based suggestions to make it happen. That makes for a great book."

Bishop Millicent Hunter
Baptist Worship Center
Philadelphia, PA

"Navigating the murky and often uncharted waters of this most intriguing millennium requires constant exposure to prophetic insight and apostolic impartation. In his newest work, *In the Grip of His Mercy,* Bishop Donald Hilliard Jr. provides the reader both of these critical components while issuing a simultaneous summons and clarion challenge to take responsibility for, and change, our pathway to destiny!"

Bishop Harold Calvin Ray
Redemptive Life Fellowship
West Palm Beach, FL

"Too often faith becomes simply sentimental and although it comforts in the good times, it cannot withstand the pressures of the bad times. In this important book, Bishop Donald Hilliard has his finger on a compelling fact of our lives today—we live under enormous pressures and pressure, as anyone knows, causes cracks in the weak places. Instead of holding on to the false hope that we are strong enough to withstand the multitude of pressures that bear down on us, Bishop Hilliard points us to the only source of hope strong enough to hold fast—the merciful and loving God we know in Jesus Christ. By his Holy Spirit, we like those Biblical figures that serve as Bishop Hilliard's case studies, can claim a new day for our lives with our hope squarely 'in the grip of His mercy.'"

The Rev. Dr. Christian Scharen
Associate Director
Yale Center for Faith and Culture
Yale Divinity School

"The pragmatic approach of *In the Grip of His Mercy* is an encouraging tool of inspiration for believers to armor up . . . be strong . . . and cling to the Heavenly Father's Love."

Bishop George G. Bloomer
Senior Pastor
Bethel Family Worship Center

"*In the Grip of His Mercy* is a much-needed resource for the Body of Christ. So often, we are distracted from the plan of God for our lives because we don't anticipate challenges before they arrive. Through this book, Bishop Hilliard will not only prepare you for the midnight hour, but also equip you to press through until joy comes in the morning!"

Pastor Paula White
Paula White Ministries

$\mathscr{I}$N THE

$\mathscr{G}$RIP OF $\mathscr{H}$IS

$\mathscr{M}$ERCY

Bishop Donald Hilliard Jr.

Introduction by
Bishop Eddie Long

Health Communications, Inc.
Deerfield Beach, Florida

www.hcibooks.com

All scripture quotations, unless otherwise indicated, are taken from the New King James Version (NKJV), copyright ©1982, Thomas Nelson Publishers. Scriptures also taken from the King James Version (KJV).

Library of Congress Cataloging-in-Publication Data

Hilliard, Donald.
    In the grip of His mercy / Donald Hilliard, Jr. ; introduction by Eddie Long.
        p. cm.
    Includes bibliographical references.
    ISBN 0-7573-0264-5
    1. Christian life. I. Title.

BV4501.3.H555 2005
248.4—dc22

200406099

©2005 Bishop Donald Hilliard Jr.
ISBN 0-7573-0264-5

All rights reserved. Printed in the United States of America. No part of this publication may be reproduced, stored in a retrieval system or transmitted in any form or by any means, electronic, mechanical, photocopying, recording or otherwise, without the written permission of the publisher.

HCI, its Logos and Marks are trademarks of Health Communications, Inc.

Publisher: Health Communications, Inc.
            3201 S.W. 15th Street
            Deerfield Beach, FL 33442-8190

Cover design by Larissa Hise Henoch
Inside book design by Lawna Patterson Oldfield
Inside book formatting by Dawn Von Strolley Grove

Dedicated to the greater glory of God,
and to those who are determined to press
through the pressures of life—either through it all,
or in spite of it all.

"Hope deferred makes the heart sick,
but a longing fulfilled is a tree of life."
Proverbs 13:12, NIV

"Life for me ain't been no crystal stair."
Langston Hughes

"We are troubled on every side, yet not distressed;
we are perplexed, but not in despair."
2 Corinthians 4:8, KJV

Contents

Foreword

Across the landscape of Christendom, worship centers are packed and pews dotted with people straining to spot any expression of the goodness of God in their lives. From coast to coast, consumer-driven believers wait for the One who made them to give a reason to tell Him "thank you," as though God were as good and worthy as the last sign/wonder in their lives . . . as though the demonstrated ability of God that's consistent with the believers' expectations is a condition for desiring and maintaining relationship with God. The goodness of God has become the wind in our sail, transporting us to ports of destiny eagerly sought. However, many have experienced shipwreck and others have gone overboard not because the wind ceased, but because no one knew which way to steer the helm.

Advance—be still, hold on—let go, Jesus will fix it—use what's in your hands and work it out. . . . Accurately identifying the divine directive for the moment is a must! We go in circles, becoming dizzier and more frustrated with each cycle because we look for, long for blessing instead of direction. Discerning the will of God wraps the mind in sanity, holds the heart in comfort, keeps the spirit in peace ever declaring to the soul all is well. Whether dawn, noon or midnight, direction from the voice that wakes the living dead and commands light to shine in darkness is indispensable.

Praise and worship we know. Prayer and fasting we know. Faith and prosperity we know. Healing and deliverance we know. Purpose, destiny and inheritance we know. But where to plant our feet when the earth beneath them is shaking we don't know. Would to God we'd court the Holy Spirit as Guide with the same fervor and affection we do the Holy Spirit as Power. The Holy Spirit as revealer of and guide into the will of God is irreplaceable in any season of life.

This book will ignite hope and stir faith so you'll never forget that, regardless of your circumstances, God's will is still current concerning you. Through these pages, you'll see that the will of God doesn't have to be a mystery even when you don't have a clue what's going on. Bishop Hilliard's compelling style and depth of conviction lace every word, summoning every reader to trust and lend an ear to the One who still speaks from eternity. Ruler of wind and wave, Jesus the Christ of God has something to say to you. Hear Him!

B. Glover-Williams, D. Min.
Executive Pastor, Cathedral International
Perth Amboy, New Jersey

Acknowledgments

I am extremely grateful to the many people who helped me with this project. One would think that after publishing four books, I would have finally . . . at long last got the hang of it. This has been a tremendous journey—and this book should have gone to press some time ago. I am nevertheless thankful to God for His grace in finishing this book, and I am confident that it will prove to be a source of strength and courage to all who read it. I am most grateful to the Reverend Larry Walker, Larry Walker Associates, Mr. Bill Carpenter and Mr. Lawrence Jordan, of the Lawrence Jordan Agency, for their editorial genius. Ms. Monee McGuire, Ms. Raquel Muniz and Minister Paula Simone Hankerson proved most helpful in copying, mailing and keeping track of my projects. Minister Christopher Michael Jones has been most helpful as my personal assistant, serving as a liaison along with Lawrence Jordan, connecting the dots. Thanks to Dr. Glover-Williams for sharing the foreword and her encouragement. Finally, I am grateful to my family. My mother, Alease Hilliard-Chapman, who after all of these years still gets as excited over special events in my life as she did when I was a young boy. My beloved wife of twenty-three years, Phyllis, my precious children, Leah, Charisma and Destiny, and my nephew Donald Robert for providing me an exuberating, warm and loving safe harbor: a place to come in from out of the cold and to feel valued and affirmed. For them I praise the Lord.

Introduction

Don't sleep. Pressure can hem you up without you even knowing it. I'm not talking about the grueling, larger-than-life pressures that are in your face. It's obvious that these hard-hitters can take us out if we succumb. But it's what I would call the quiet, quick pressures that catch us off guard and can also wreak havoc. Look at Adam. When Eve presented him with the apple, he knew what God told him. But he didn't speak up. He didn't stand up for God. In that quick moment, he gave into pressure and was more inclined to please his wife than he was to please God. So he ate the fruit, and as a result, we experienced the fall of man.

We must remind ourselves often that life's pressures come in all shapes and sizes. Some carry us around the bend; others take us straight through the fire. There are major tragedies and day-to-day decisions. We fight against the enemy's warfare and press through God's trials. But whatever the challenge, when we remember that pressures can strike at any time and in any form, we are more apt to "stay awake" and constantly prepare ourselves for any and all encounters to come. Constant preparation comes by reading, internalizing and putting into practice the Word of God; it's the claim to victory that is the same through all circumstances. It gives us what we need to stand and press through.

For many, it doesn't take much more than hearing someone else's situation to discover that things in *your* world *could* be much worse. But when you're in the middle of what seems to be hell on earth, sometimes your focus gets stripped away and you get sucked in to feeling sorry for yourself, complaining, running away, or giving up altogether. During these times, it's difficult to even hold your head up, much less stand. But in the midst of struggle, if we could just recall the words "Caleb" and "Joshua." Then, if we could remember that we need to have an attitude like them—an attitude of perseverance, commitment and an air of boldness—then we will be guided through the seasons. This attitude will dictate that no matter what you see in front of you or around you, you've elected to follow God. You've committed to learn or remember what His word says about your circumstances and about life. You've opted not to fall prey to the negative pressures, but rather to be of a different spirit, embedding His promises in your heart. I'm not denying that you may get weak. I am simply saying that your strength undoubtedly lies in Him.

If you're struggling through a situation right now, you need this book. If all is well with you right now, you *definitely* need this book to prepare for what's to come! No matter where you are in life, *In the Grip of His Mercy* gives you the inspiration to armor up, be strong and get busy learning how to cling to the Heavenly Father's love. Trials and tribulations will surely come, but they come and go. What remains is that God *still* has His perfect plan for your life.

My friend, this book has blessed me. I pray that it takes you to another level in Christ.

—Bishop Eddie L. Long
Senior Pastor
New Birth Missionary Baptist Church
Lithonia, GA

1

Living in the Grip of Mercy

As you read these words, some mother's precious child is kneeling in a "shooting gallery" in a major U.S. metropolis with a hypodermic needle in her hand. In her desperation, she doesn't care that she is shooting another part of her life away with every injection of crack cocaine into her veins.

Another mother's child pickles his brains with cheap liquor, "crystal meth" and prescription pills from Dad's medicine cabinet in a small Midwestern town.

Someone is walking down Wilshire Boulevard in Los Angeles but glamour is the last thing on her mind. The battered supermarket cart she pushes tells the story—it contains all of her worldly possessions and most of what remains of her memories.

The sun may be shining, but day or night, another soul in Detroit wears four winter overcoats and three wool caps layered in the misbegotten fashion common to victims of absolute poverty and the bankruptcy of personality. The look hasn't changed in thirty days, and he will keep wearing those clothes until they fall off of his body, are stolen in the night by another who is stronger than him or until he dies in them.

People like these are rarely born into such bankruptcy—at least, not in America—but somewhere along life's journey, under the pressures of life, something inside them snapped. This explains why our urban skid-row populations always seem to include some of the leaders of yesterday. These fallen stockbrokers, attorneys, architects and surgeons share tales of the pressures that finally toppled them from the ranks of the elite and the respectable. Those pressures somehow landed them in the human trash heap reserved for the last remains and remnants of society's fabric. Each of them carries painful memories of a shattered dream, a missed opportunity or an unfulfilled hope.

Whatever brought these individuals from where they were to where they are today, I have to say there is a better way.

Some of life's victims have never ventured onto the dark streets of an inner-city ghetto. The panic and anguish that come with poverty or true hunger are totally foreign to them, yet the pressures surging against their lives are just as lethal.

Often we hear of someone with a loaded gun pointed toward his sweaty forehead, anguishing over a rush of desperate thoughts racing for final expression before a shaking finger pulls the trigger on his life. He was "brought up right." He grew up in the church and taught Sunday school to kids. "How could this happen?" his distraught parents and family members cry. Each of them carries painful memories of a shattered dream.

Pressure: The Issue of the
New Millennium

Did these victims of life's pressure points ever hear the good news about God's love for them? Did they hear it but dismiss the messenger and the message as mere religious propaganda, with no power to heal what hurts on the inside?

For whatever reason, when faced with the mounting pressures of life, victims helplessly succumb instead of fighting to press through them to find freedom and new strength.

Pressure is the issue of the new millennium for most Americans. We are learning that life's journey is similar to our first journey from the womb into the world. In this odd mix of tenderness and violence, the birth process thrusts unceremoniously from the comfort of our climate-controlled home with all the amenities into the narrow confines of the birth canal.

Along the way we must negotiate a highly traumatic "pressure point" where the mother's bone structure encourages us to turn and press through just so before we can see the light of day. Most of us negotiate this passage headfirst, but some of us just have to make our start in life by "backing our way" into the light.

Life on the "outside" presents us with yet another series of pressure points, or what may be called birthing places. When we encounter these points, we can stall the birth process and die stillborn; we can take a detour and be forcibly removed from where we are at great risk; or we can press through the temporary pain of the pressure point to a new beginning.

King David of ancient Israel knew about pressure. He discovered firsthand what pressure can do to an otherwise faithful man.

Pressure Can Lead Even the Best of Us to Do the Worst Things

David is, without question, one of the greatest leaders of the Bible and indeed of human history. Yet, this fierce warrior, poet without equal and future king nevertheless found himself, because of the pressures of life, identifying with an ancient enemy.

This enemy—an aggressive coastal people called the Philistines—was one of the most persistent oppressors of the Israelites. It was David's dramatic defeat of a Philistine warrior named Goliath that first catapulted him into Israel's public eye.[1] So how did Israel's great champion end up siding with his bitter enemies?

Pressure can lead even the best of men and women to do the worst things imaginable if they fail to overcome it.

David was running for his life to avoid King Saul and the Israelite army. In a rage fueled by jealously and envy, Saul sought David's life. All David really wanted in Saul, however, was a father, a mentor. Even with this rage against him, David never retaliated—declaring that Saul was still the Lord's anointed. It was the pressure of running and hiding from Saul day and night that caused David to seek asylum and protection in the house of his enemies. When David took his army of six hundred men into Philistia to escape Saul, Achish, the Philistine king of Gath, gave

David the city of Ziklag—a Judean city under Philistine control. David and his men lived in Ziklag with their families for a total of sixteen months.[2] In return for this favor, David was to fight for the Philistines when asked.

Pressure had prodded the future king of Israel to seek asylum with and pay rent to Israel's most hated enemy. But even this uneasy truce between enemies fell apart the day the Philistines decided to attack King Saul and the Israelite army. Fearing that David and his men would turn on them in the middle of the fight, the Philistine commanders told David to turn around and go back to Ziklag.[3]

Has pressure ever made you do something that you regret? Pressure can make you marry the wrong person. If you are not careful, pressure can make you sign a contract before you read the dangerous details in fine print. Pressure can make you feel you have to do something by a certain time.

As a pastor, I've lost count of the number of people who have told me in counseling that they lost everything because they made a hasty and bad decision out of pressure. Some of them went to the altar and pledged eternal vows of matrimony out of pressure—and lived to regret it. Pressure led others to become involved with activities, associations and business relationships that they viewed as wrong.

David Knew Pain

Back in Ziklag, David and his men encountered even more pressure:

> *Now it happened, when David and his men came to Ziklag, on the third day, that the Amalekites had invaded the South and Ziklag, attacked Ziklag and burned it with fire, and had taken captive the women and those who were there, from small to great; they did not kill anyone, but carried them away and went their way. So David and his men came to the city, and there it was, burned with fire; and their wives, their sons, and their daughters had been taken captive. Then David and the people who were with him lifted up their voices and wept, until they had no more power to weep. (1 Sam. 30:1–4)*

David knew the language of pain. He knew what it was like to cry and then cry some more until the tears no longer flowed. Yet as bad as things were for David, they were about to get even worse. The Bible tells us that while David was grieving over the kidnapping of his wives, more trouble was brewing: "Now David was greatly distressed, *for the people spoke of stoning him,* because the soul of all the people was grieved, every man for his sons and his daughters. . . . "[4] This sentence contains far more power than most casual readers will ever know.

David Faced a Crisis
of Lethal Proportions

The Bible says David was "greatly distressed," and the original Hebrew word literally means "to press, be narrow," or to "be in distress, to be distressed, to be in a narrow place or to be in narrow straits, and to be vexed."[5] Doesn't that sound exactly like the "birth canal" experience we just examined? But this was more than mere distress—this was a crisis of lethal proportions!

David was in deep trouble, even for a man who was used to living in harm's way. Saul, the king of Israel, had spoken a death sentence over him and unleashed Israel's army to hunt him down. Then David's temporary shelter among the Philistines had evaporated when they began fighting with Israel again. When David and his men finally reached the city of Ziklag in Judea, they thought their families would be waiting for them but instead saw smoke rising from what was left of their burned-out homes.

Now the very men who had risked death to stay with David were ready to stone him! Right or wrong, they blamed him for the bad things that had happened to their wives and children. That meant David had to cope with their rejection of him and their dangerous threats while also trying to cope with his own grief over the loss of his wives. David was out of options, choices and resources. There was no place to run—except one. The Scripture tells us that at this dire pressure point what David did was to turn to the one sure source of strength in danger. ". . . But David strengthened himself in the LORD his God."[6]

The apostle Paul was another man who knew what it was like to encounter the pressures of life. In his second letter to the early Christians in ancient Corinth, he wrote,

> *But we have this treasure in earthen vessels, that the excellence of the power may be of God and not of us.* We are hard pressed on every side, *yet not crushed; we are perplexed, but not in despair;* persecuted, *but not forsaken; struck down, but not destroyed,* always carrying about in the body the dying of the Lord Jesus, *that the life of Jesus also may be manifested in our body. (2 Cor. 4:7–10, emphasis mine)*

Pressure—crushing, suffocating, bloodying pressure—was a reality in Paul's life, but he refused to be dominated or hindered by it. For a Christian, life is a process of learning how to press beyond life's pressure points through Christ. But too many of us take shortcuts or detours in this learning process, and if you are not careful, life's pressure points can do you in.

Pressure Does Not Have to Be Your Undoing!

I believe you picked up this book precisely because you have personally experienced what it is like to be on the other side of hope. You have tasted the bitter seeds of disappointment, and you know how it feels to be broken. Everyone knows what it is like to be bruised and misused, but you may also know what it is like to be abused in one way or another.

May I suggest to you that pressure does not have to be your undoing? Pressure can become your greatest launching point to a great future—but only if you follow David into the secret place of the Most High; only if you strengthen yourself in the Lord your God.

As you read these words, you may be struggling for air or grappling with an impossible situation that threatens to take you under. If you are, take a moment now to lift up your head, breathe a prayer of thanksgiving and praise to Jesus Christ and declare out loud:

> *I will not let pressure get the best of me! I will not lose my mind. I will not let my blood pressure rise to the point of stroke level simply because misdirected people have crossed the path of my life. I will allow pressure to build me, to develop me, and to strengthen me—but it will not destroy me!*

God Still Loves the Fool Who's Playing the Part

Have you ever tried to run from God or to avoid a divine assignment? I must tell you that even in your worst moments, even when you try to run from God, He still loves you. He doesn't condone our foolish actions, but He sure loves the fool who's playing the part. You knew it was wrong; you shouldn't have gone. You knew you were in the wrong place at the wrong time with the wrong people, but you were angry with God and felt like He "owed it to you." Perhaps you felt you deserved to walk on the wild side just for one night. . . .

If you are a Christian, I can almost finish the story for you. Somebody came up to you along the way to say, "You don't belong here. Why don't you go on back where you came from? You're just messing up the party. You don't know how to lean on the bar anymore. You just don't fit in with us." Why does this happen? Because deep down on the inside, even though you chose to temporarily turn your back on God, God did not turn His back on you. Now, you should not consider this as an invitation to sin—we will still have to account for our actions one day—but do consider it as a tribute to God's faithfulness in the face of our foolishness.

The pressure of fear prodded Peter to deny that he even knew Jesus on three different occasions. He was unnerved when the people around him just kept probing and questioning him: "Aren't you one of His disciples? You look like one of them. Your accent gives you away."

My friend, once you have identified with Christ, you will begin to look, smell and sound like Him in some mysterious way. It seems that most people can tell if you have *really* been touched by God—even though you may temporarily be in a backslidden state. It doesn't matter whether you are hiding at the dark end of a hotel bar or running from Nineveh on a sailing ship, God's hand is still on you.

Survival in the Grip of Mercy

You may have stepped out of a bed of fornication or adultery on Saturday night, but then found yourself sliding into the back pew of your church on Sunday morning. All you know is that something keeps calling you back into the church and drawing you to the altar.

Make no mistake: You are in the grip of the mercy of God. Pressure can make you identify with wrong, but the power of God that is inside you will wake you up and cause you to identify with right. God does more than say, "Sin is wrong." He gets involved and helps you overcome it.

David came face-to-face with even more pressure when he made his way back to Ziklag. This became David's personal city of fire and place of pressure. He was threatened, dejected, dismissed and at risk. He was disappointed beyond expression and depressed by everything he saw: his house burned, his children gone, his wives kidnapped by his bitter enemies, the Amalekites. His own men even wanted to stone him to death on the spot. The God who got him into all this must have seemed far away at that moment. I wonder if David was tempted to say, "So much for Samuel's great prophecy about me being king of Israel!"

This man was facing the life-crushing pressure of *multiple crises,* the kind of pressure that can lead some to prematurely end their own lives or to give up their most cherished dreams and callings.

The pressure of multiple crises can quickly get the best of us if we are unprepared to cope with it or are spiritually unstable. Most of us can handle one pressure at a time, but when one thing after another goes wrong, when we are faced with multiple traumas, we are tempted to try to stop the struggle in the middle of the "birth canal."

Something happens on the job at the same time as something is going wrong in your marriage. Your doctor finds a lump in your colon or breast, and when you get in the car to drive home, your engine blows up. When you arrive late for work the next morning, your boss fires you. That night your son brings home a failing report card and your daughter announces she is pregnant by her seventeen-year-old boyfriend. Any two of these crises could trigger a meltdown in anyone who does not have access to spiritual resources.

There must be an inner source of power, something within. Oh, how I would love to hear the late Evelyn Faison sing in the early days of my pastorate, "Something within me, Holdeth the reign, Something within me, Vanquishes pain, Something within me, I cannot explain, All that I know, Is there is Something within. . . ." It's this inner Power that keeps us steady and sane.

Stretched on the "Rack of Ziklag"

Pressure can be your undoing, or it can become your tutor. For David, pressure marked the entrance into a divine season of preparation. God was preparing David for something of eternal importance. The day would come when he would lead far more than six hundred men, and the stakes would be much higher than the loss of a few houses.

David was being stretched on the rack of Ziklag. His desert "birth canal" was reshaping and conforming him to a higher, holier and mightier image of himself than the one he had previously held.

God used the Devil's calamity to transport David into a position of heavenly grace. The Heavenly Father was preparing His shepherd boy for the throne.

Let me reassure you that God loves you too, and He is not the author of the bad things that come your way. He may *allow* the pressures of life to form and conform you to His divine image, but He never intends for life's pressure points to destroy you. Remember what another biblical hero, Joseph, told his brothers about their evil plot to sell him to slave traders: "You meant evil against me; but God meant it for good, in order to bring it about as it is this day, to save many people alive."[7] Joseph saw and understood that when we allow God into our lives, He can turn a bad situation to a good purpose. David's pressure points had prepared him well for his divine destiny in life. People who demonstrate God's power in their everyday lives and in service to others know what it is like to cry through the night, or to have a figurative dagger stuck in their backs. Virtually every genuinely anointed person in God's kingdom knows something about *disappointment*. There really is no progress without pain.

But struggle produces strength. Olympic champions are not born and developed in the lap of leisure; they rise to the top of athletic competition through *struggle*. This is thoroughly biblical. "Beloved, think it not strange concerning the fiery trial which is to try you, as though some strange thing happened unto you."[8]

When your bills outrun your money, don't stop giving to the Lord. That's the time to *start giving more*. Continue giving your tithe, expand your faith and plant a breakthrough offering. Don't stop talking to God when things go wrong; start praying even more.

In those dark hours when you feel beaten down and hopeless in heart, lift your eyes away from your problems, raise your hands in praise and shout "Glory to God!" with all of the volume and determination you can muster. Declare boldly, "I will lift up mine eyes unto the hills from whence cometh my strength. My help comes from the Lord."

Why? Because God inhabits the praises of His people. And because He has promised that in times of trouble, He shall hide and comfort us.

Disturbers of the Peace

Have you ever noticed that every church seems to have a certain number of people who can't seem to stay quiet? If you try to have a serene service with the soft reading of a psalm, you might be able to stifle all the singers. That is, until somebody—someone with an unquenchable fount of joy—just has to break out with some expression of praise or worship that "disturbs" that silent atmosphere.

I am thankful for these divinely inspired disturbers of the peace. These Holy Ghost prompters don't need to be encouraged to worship. They *can't help themselves* because most of them know what it means to go through trials and tribulation and to come out on the other end with victory in their hands.

They've learned the secret of worshipping God with *all* their heart, soul, mind and strength. They aren't interested in being caught up in church decorum. David said exactly what they *feel*: "I was glad when they said unto me, Let us go into the house of the LORD."[9]

David seemed to live most of his early life in one long season of preparation. David was a *teenager* the day God's prophet Samuel anointed him to be king of Israel.[10] Even with the prophecy from the man of God, David didn't actually receive the crown of Israel until he was thirty years old![11]

What happened in the meantime? David went through what we call an apprenticeship. God was preparing His chosen leader to rule and reign.

David experienced these seasons of pressure for a reason, and it wasn't very pleasant at times. *Your* suffering may not seem very encouraging at the moment either, but God is preparing you to rule and reign also. You are victorious!

"God Is Testing the Hell out of Me!"

I remember visiting one of the ladies in my church who was going through an incredible series of trials with her marriage, her children, her job and the loss of loved ones. After listening to her story, I said, "Daughter, the Lord is just bringing you through." Then I took her hand and began to pray with her: "God, strengthen her. Lord, touch her." Then I added, "He's just testing you. He's teaching and developing you." At that point this dear Christian woman said, "Let me just say one thing, Bishop: *God is testing the hell out of me, and I just wish He'd stop it!*"

That caught me off guard, but after a moment of thought I said, "Yes, God is testing the hell out of you, Sister; and He's testing the hell out of me too, because when He gets finished, there won't be any more hell left on the inside of us. God is making us sweeter, kinder and more prayerful. He's making us into praisers."

We all face pressures in a society still divided along the lines of gender, race and religion. To make things even worse, our society is growing increasingly cold. We are becoming a high-tech, low-touch society where few people genuinely seem to care for others. At times it seems difficult to know who we can trust.

If you are not careful, you can let people put a ceiling on your blessing; you can let them block your march to destiny and the crown God has promised you. You have to look past the critics and hypocrites, and say yes to God.

God told the prophet Jeremiah, "When you prophesy, *don't even look at the people.*"[13] I learned that lesson years ago. At times my mother would ask me, "Who are you preaching to? Who are you looking at when you preach?"

"I'm preaching to the air," I told her. "If I can't find a friendly face and a confirming glance in the audience, then I'll just preach to thin air if I have to. If no one receives the Word of the Lord, then I'll just put hands on my own head and proclaim His truth to myself if necessary." You must refuse to be hindered by negativity and people whose intentions are mean and resentful.

The Bible tells us, "And whatsoever ye do, do it heartily, as to the Lord."[14] That means a singer should sing until the wallpaper begins to peel off the walls, if necessary. Sing until the glory of God comes down!

God Wants Us to Trust Solely in Him

This God of power and might has to become *your* God, not just "Momma's God" or "the preacher's God." He must become for you "a pillar of cloud by day and a pillar of fire by night," as He was during the exodus for the ancient Israelites. He must become your Rock, your Provider, your Hope, and your personal Lord and Savior. He wants to do more than simply save you from hellfire. He is interested in every detail of your life. He is the One who has planted great dreams in your heart.

God is trying to raise up a people who trust solely in Him. Sometimes He will allow the props in your life to be misplaced because you have begun to lean on them instead of on Him. You have started to put your trust and hope in the wrong things. Some trust in alcohol and drugs, success and money or the size of their real estate portfolios. There are those who trust in their looks and physical strength. "Some trust in chariots, and some in horses"; the psalmist declares, "But we will remember the name of the LORD our God."[15] Indeed: "The name of the LORD is a strong tower; the righteous run to it and are safe."[16]

David built up and encouraged himself in the Lord *his* God. In the middle of his darkest hour, David said to himself, "I will *bless* the Lord!" He was determined to worship God and to turn his attention from the direness of his situation. He put his focus on the Supreme Solution to every problem when he declared in his pain, "I will bless the LORD at all times: his praise shall continually be in my mouth."[17] In other words, he was saying:

"God, I'll praise You in the good times and the bad, when I'm up and when I'm down. I will bless You whether I'm popular or unpopular, whether I have money in my pocket or not a dime to my name. In every situation, I will bless You."

Later in his life, after pressing through a lifetime of pressure points, David was able to write, with the confidence of hard-won wisdom, "I have been young, and now am old; yet I have not seen the righteous forsaken, nor his descendants begging bread."[18]

The greatest revenge against the adversary of our souls—and those who seem to delight in helping him do his dirty work in our lives—is simply to stand fast in the face of pressure, without backing up or giving up. Too often we waste precious time trying to get back at our enemies. We would do well to remember "Vengeance is mine saith the Lord." Ultimately, we all reap what we sow. Don't waste time trying to get even; finish what you started, hold your head up high and go forth. At the end of the day you can testify that "I'm still here!" Your challenge is to press through life's pressure points and take joy in the fact that you are still here. You have survived!

It pleases God and brings Him glory when you refuse to fold under the pressure of ruthless criticism, when you say no to the doubters and naysayers who hate and fear your God-given dreams. Joseph, the dreamer of the Old Testament, was hated by his own brothers simply because he had a dream. Could it be that dreamers are a threat to those who have no dreams or those who look back with regret over missed opportunities and dine on bitterness and regret? It would do us all well to dwell among those who wish us well and celebrate us rather than berate us. Life is too short to waste time trying to convince dream killers that dreams really do come true.

You will survive if you hold your head up high, square your shoulders, lift your hands and give God praise in the midst of your darkest hour. Do it, and watch Him raise you up in front of your enemies. For no matter how bad things look, those who live in the grip of mercy will always win.

— Endnotes ————————————————————

[1] Sam. 17.

[2] Sam. 27:2–7.

[3] Sam. 29:1–11.

[4] Sam. 30:6, italics mine.

[5] James Strong, *Strong's Exhaustive Concordance of the Bible* (Peabody, MA: Hendrickson Publishers, n.d.); meanings and definitions drawn from the word derivations for **distressed** (Hebrew, #3334).

[6] 1 Sam. 30:6b.

[7] Gen. 50:20.

[8] 1 Pet. 4:12 KJV.

[9] Ps. 122:1.

[10] 1 Sam. 16:11–13.

[11] 2 Samuel 5:4.

[12] Rev. 1:6 and 5:10.

[13] Jer. 1:17, my paraphrase and emphasis.

[14] Col. 3:23 KJV.

[15] Ps. 20:7.

[16] Prov. 18:10.

[17] Ps. 34:1b.

[18] Ps. 37:25.

2

The Call to Produce

A fruit orchard never looks more forlorn than in the period following a growing season. If you drive past the carefully aligned rows of fruit trees, you will see occasional gaps. Wherever you find a gap, you also may see a pile of exposed roots and the withered branches of a tree unceremoniously uprooted from the ground. These displaced and discarded trees failed to achieve their potential in previous fruit-bearing seasons. The places in the orchard they once occupied become seedbeds for the fresh potential of new trees. As for the withered remnants of the uprooted trees, they are sometimes chipped and converted into mulch to nourish other living things or are simply gathered together and burned.

Jesus understood the dynamics of orchards, fruit groves and fruit-bearing trees. Several times in the Gospels, He taught parables of instruction rooted in the life cycle and purpose of the fig tree. In one story, a barren fig tree was cursed for failing to bear fruit,[1] but in another, a barren fig tree is given a second chance.

> *A certain man had a fig tree planted in his vineyard, and he came seeking fruit on it and found none. Then he said to the keeper of his vineyard, "Look, for three years I have come seeking fruit on this fig tree and find none. Cut it down; why does it use up the ground?" But he answered and said to him, "Sir, let it alone this year also, until I dig around it and fertilize it." (Luke 13:6–8)*

Some of the pressures we encounter in life are actually good for us. The Creator designed the fig tree to survive the rigors of new growth as a sapling, to survive high winds and seasons of drought. Yet, He designed it to do more than merely survive—He created it to produce figs. This fruit protects the seed of the tree and is the means by which the tree reproduces itself and perpetuates its line in a new generation!

In difficult seasons it is quite an accomplishment just to survive, but most of the time it isn't good enough for you and me to merely survive. God created us to thrive! When we produce fruit, we reproduce ourselves and perpetuate our voice in His Kingdom. Too many of us think we have accomplished our destiny when, rescued from certain eternal death on the road of life, we run to our Rescuer and say, "Thank You, Jesus—You saved my life!"

His surprising reply is simply, "Good! *Now make My death count for something in your life. Help Me save others just like you.*"

That kind of godly pressure is meant for good and not for evil. It is a forward pressure to fulfill our destiny and divine purpose.

God wants you to look back at the seasons of your life and say, "By God's grace, my life has been a continuous series of fruitful seasons. Isn't God good?" Sadly, if we were truthful, far too many of us would have to characterize our lives as a continuous series of wasted seasons. But no matter where we stand, the Lord's parable of the fig tree in Luke's Gospel is both a stern warning and a much-needed word of grace.

A Second Chance

When I compare the two main fig tree parables—the one in which the fig tree is cursed and the one where it is given a second chance—my personal favorite is at least partially based on my own need. I haven't reached perfection yet (and neither has anyone else I've met so far in life). That means I have an almost unlimited need for grace to cover my imperfections and continual failures in life.

The unfruitful fig tree in Luke 13 had a long-term problem, not some "overnight crisis" produced by a great and sudden challenge, obstacle or risk. This is a parable about the unproductiveness rooted in laziness and chronic apathy rather than the disorienting influence of outside forces. This fruitless fig tree had nothing and no one else to blame for its lack of production.

Despite the tree's three years of failure to produce figs, the vinedresser convinced the vineyard owner to give the tree one more season to produce fruit. There is no doubt about the matter: That tree should have been bearing fruit and "earning its keep" in the vineyard, but it wasn't. When it failed to fulfill its purpose for existence, by all rights it should have been cut down. Instead, it was given one more season of opportunity to bear fruit.

I don't know about you, but when I look at what I have accomplished thus far in my life and compare it with the list of things God has placed in my heart, I am quick to confess to Him, "Lord, I need another opportunity. Please give me another season."

I suspect that most of us need another opportunity to make the most of our lives. Thankfully, we serve a God of infinite grace and mercy, a Creator and heavenly Father who is always trying to infiltrate our situation, to get our attention. Why does He do this? So we won't keep making the same mistakes over and over again.

I believe that the Lord wants us to understand the seasons of the spirit and the role of divine timing in planting and reaping for the kingdom of God.

Give Me One More Season

I haven't reached my maximum potential yet. When I consider what Jesus said about the unfruitful fig tree, I want to cry out, "Give me one more season, Lord. I want to make this next season right by putting into action what I have learned."

Daniel said that God "changes the times and the seasons; He

removes kings and raises up kings; He gives wisdom to the wise
and knowledge to those who have understanding."² And David,
in his celebrated first psalm, reveals some secrets for having fruitful seasons in God's "earthly orchard":

> *Blessed is the man who walks not in the counsel of the ungodly, nor
> stands in the path of sinners, nor sits in the seat of the scornful; but
> his delight is in the law of the LORD, and in His law he meditates
> day and night. He shall be like a tree planted by the rivers of water,
> that brings forth its fruit in its season, whose leaf also shall not wither;
> and whatever he does shall prosper. (Ps. 1:1–3)*

Christians who are bearing the fruit of their faith don't have
hit-and-miss lives marked by occasional spurts of spiritual inspiration. They don't have to blow off the dust accumulated on
their Bibles when they sit down to read them. Without exception, you will discover that they have consistent relationships
with God and that they continuously communicate with Him
throughout the day and in the night hours.

A Promise to Live By

Don't allow excessive familiarity with the words to rob you of
the rich truth found in Psalm 1. Look closely at that passage
again and take David's words to heart. David says that the person who takes the time to know God will be like a tree planted
by a river. That person's life will produce fruit in its season and

his or her "leaf" (or life) will not wither from lack of water. Furthermore, David says *whatever that person does* will *prosper.* If God is God, and if His Word is true (and He *is* God and His Word *is* true), then this is a promise you can live by!

Whether we realize it or not, we are reaping things today that were sown years ago—some of them good and some of them evil. When I need to unwind and relax, I head for my garden. Several years ago I set out to make a flower bed in my garden, but after I had already planted the flower seeds, I changed my mind and planted vegetables in that area.

My plan was to remove the flower seeds and put them in another part of the yard later. Unfortunately, that particular later never came, but something else did. I forgot about my season of mixed sowing until I noticed the vegetables and flowers emerging from the soil together.

Even though I had forgotten what I had planted, in due season I reaped a harvest of tomatoes, cucumbers and other vegetables along with a brilliant mix of garden flowers. It didn't matter that I had forgotten what I had sown. The bottom line is that I reaped what I had sown. So it is in life.

Today, we enjoy blessings for which we asked God years ago; we also struggle with the harvest of yesterday's seeds of neglect, avoidance, laziness or outright rebellion against God's calling for us. Forgotten or not, your harvest from yesterday's seeds will surely come.

What Fruit Do God's People Bear?

A fruitful season in the life of a mature Christian is evident in both the spiritual and natural realms. As I grow in God, I should begin to produce outward proof —the fruit of God's presence in my life.[3] Everyone who works, lives or worships near me should see a consistent "harvest" of love, joy, peace, long-suffering, kindness, goodness, faithfulness, gentleness and self-control. That doesn't mean we won't have our "human moment" from time to time, but those moments of anger, unkindness or loss of self-control should be the exception rather than the rule. So often our trees simply don't bear fruit because they're planted in the wrong soil, or they become contaminated by the environment they are planted in.

As the Spirit of Christ gains preeminence, or first place, in my life, I shouldn't have to be wrestling with uncontrollable mood swings day after day. My behavior should exhibit peace and joy, even through the ups and downs that come with life on earth.

If I am in a fruitful season and if I take fruit bearing seriously, then I should be "reproducing after my own kind." In other words, I should be bringing people into the kingdom of God because I am a believer. As Proverbs declares, "The fruit of the righteous is a tree of life; and he that winneth souls is wise."[4] If I am a fruitful Christian, then I should be able to point to other people I have led to Christ, because I took the kingdom seriously enough to bring them in. That is the spiritual truth I'm talking about.

Indeed, there should be evidence of divine favor in my life. Far too many of us wear poverty and hopelessness like a tailor-made garment, when we were born to fulfill our destiny and reach our potential. Yes, prosperity is in our bones.

I believe that the biblical concept of returning one's tithes to the Lord and sharing offerings are keys to prosperity. It is critically important to be disciplined in one's financial matters. It is equally important to give back to others. As these disciplines become lifestyle choices, we should move well beyond living from hand to mouth and always being a day late and a dollar short financially. Yes, financial challenges will come, but overall God's mighty hand of provision and blessing should be evident in our lives.

The apostle John said, "Beloved, I pray that you may prosper in all things and be in health, just as your soul prospers."[5] As Christians, we experience financial crises just like non-Christians, but we should not have to live from hand to mouth as a regular lifestyle. If I am living by faith under the covenants God decreed in His Word, then I should be prospering spiritually, physically and financially.

There should be another component, or focus, in my life that involves wealth accumulation for the purpose of establishing God's kingdom on earth. Wealth building involves determined debt resolution, home ownership and long-term planning and investment in trade school or a college education and graduate studies—for our children and our children's children.

If you are bearing fruit as a Christian, you should be concerned about more than just having a good time at church or attending every revival and Christian convention you can. Those things are needed and they are wonderful, but you should also ask God what you should be leaving as a legacy for those who are coming behind you.

God is personally concerned about what kind of kingdom you will leave behind. Paul's letters, written in the final days of his life and ministry, make it clear that he considered the people he touched and the churches he planted to be his greatest testimony in this life. What lasting legacy will you leave behind in the hearts and lives of your family, friends and acquaintances?

What Keeps Us from Thriving?

The vineyard owner in Jesus' parable had a problem. He came to the vineyard hoping to gather some ripe figs for a pie or some homemade fig bars; when he found nothing but leaves on the fig tree, he decided to talk to his vine keeper.

"Hey, I've been coming to the same fig tree in the same vineyard now for three years, just hoping I would find some figs someday," he said. "I know that I planted a *fig* tree, but I don't see any *figs*—after three long years. I'll tell you what, just cut the whole thing down. That thing is only taking up space. It may look like a fig tree, but real fig trees bear figs. Cut it down and plant something that *produces* for a change." I wonder if the owner of the vineyard was tempted to fire the vine keeper.

But the vine keeper asked for one more season, and he suggested several key hindrances that had to be removed. He told the vineyard owner: "I know you are sore, angry and aggravated because there is no productivity in this tree. Give me another chance, just one more fruit-bearing season so I can make some emergency changes. Give me another season so that I can dig around the root of this tree. Let me see what's going on in the root cluster. With your permission, I would like to fertilize the tree—put nutrients there that were not there before. If you will give me another year, I will invest in this tree all the accumulated lessons, knowledge and wisdom that I have received over its three years of nonproductivity."

Disease Can Rob You of Productivity

One of the things the vine keeper wanted to do was to closely check the root system of the tree for any sign of disease. Perhaps some type of disease was infiltrating the tree and hindering the growth that should have been evident by that time. We must do the same with our lives and the lives of those in our care. When a child comes home from school with poor grades over and over again, a parent knows *something* is wrong. Sometimes it is the child and sometimes it is the teacher. Some teachers don't teach well, or they fail to take into account the child's learning style.

At other times some physical problem is intervening in the child's life. If a student needs glasses and is seated in the rear of the class, poor performance is virtually guaranteed. Diseases and problems such as hearing impairment, attention deficit disorder (ADD) and dyslexia will dramatically hinder a child's ability to learn.

The vine keeper asked the owner of the vineyard for one more season to restore the fig tree to vibrant health and productivity. He knew there were diseases that work their way into the core of the tree, but he had to get to the root to discover the truth.

Some diseases in trees (and people) are easy to spot. They work from the outside in to cut off growth and productivity and to bring about destruction. The diseases that work from the inside out are perhaps more destructive because they work out of sight, underneath the bark and in the marrow of the tree. They infiltrate the underground root system and work silently and invisibly to take the life out of the tree. Their presence is undetected until you dig around the tree and visually inspect the roots or take test samples.

Human "trees" suffer from diseases too.[6] Some spiritual diseases can be spotted from a distance because of their visible symptoms. A spirit of poverty affects the outward appearance of its victims. It transforms their very countenance so that you can see the absence of hope and vision when you look into the victims' eyes, much like jaundice will turn the white portion of its victims' eyes into a bright yellow.

Secret Sins Can Destroy from Within

Other spiritual sicknesses work from within to erode the fiber of our dreams. The disease of compulsive gambling falls into this category. You can't always see the destructive effects of gambling until it is too late. The victim has to be essentially caught in the act. Too often, family members don't realize the extent of the problem until cars are repossessed, a foreclosure notice on the family home arrives by courier or someone asks what happened to the mortgage money that was in the main checking account.

Pornography is another "secret" sin that affects its victims in the same hidden ways as compulsive gambling. Pastors, elders, deacons and Sunday school teachers have all fallen into this disease of the soul while continuing to conduct their public ministries as if nothing was wrong in the core of their being. Yet all the while, a deadly and devilish disease was eroding their marriages, their ministries, their healthy relationships with others and with God.

Some diseases of the spirit are so intensely deceptive that they will cause you to believe that God Himself has led you into sin for your benefit! This is nothing other than pure self-deception. "Sin, when it is finished, bringeth forth death."[7] I've counseled women who were so lonely that they entered into adultery with another woman's husband believing that *God had sent him* to be their husband! That is deception. God will *never* lead you into sin to accomplish the works of righteousness.[8]

No matter how many ways you try to paint evil as good, it still comes out evil. If you dabble in sin, your tree will not grow or produce righteous fruit. No matter how you try to fix it, phrase it or replay it, sin is sin. To call it by any other name is deception, and it will not get you anywhere but deeper into sin.

Just Producing an Illusion

Sooner or later, a tree affected by pollution or disease will begin to rot from the inside out. The bark may still be intact on the outside and the branches may still have green leaves, producing the illusion that it is still growing. Yet eventually, one branch will fall off . . . and then another. Then the tree itself will break in half or will be uprooted when stormy winds begin to blow.

The Lord says that sin "brings forth death" when it is finished. And the only remedy for sin is the blood of the Lamb of God. Only one elixir can wash away our sin, and that is the shed blood of Jesus Christ.

If your "tree" is diseased, then a corrosive and erosive affliction is eating away at the root of your life. It is time to wake up and tell yourself, "I must deal with this disease!" Each of us must ask ourselves these questions: "Why am I not bearing fruit? Why don't I ever have any money? Why don't I own any property? Why don't I have any wealth? Why don't I have any peace of mind? Why is there no joy in my soul? Why is there no hope in my spirit?"

If you are trapped in a consuming sexual addiction, chances are that no one will know about your problem until you are caught in the middle of it somehow. It may happen at three o'clock in the morning when your wife follows the telephone cord to the closet door and hears you whispering on the phone with some faceless person you reached on an "adult" 900 number. If you are a single person, it may happen when an unwanted pregnancy exposes to the world what you have secretly been doing behind closed doors.

If you are trapped in an addictive or compulsive sin, you need to confess your sin so you can be free. If you don't confess to the truth, God loves you so much that He will see to it that you are caught in the midst of your sin, anything to get you out of the trap you are in.

The sin of lying never comes out until you're caught. As a Christian, you should know you are under the influence of a lying spirit when you can lie with a straight face as if it were second nature. Sadly, we train our children to lie when we tell them, "Tell the salesman at the door that I'm not home." When the child we've trained not to lie says, "Dad, he has probably already heard you," we answer, "It doesn't matter. Tell him I'm not home." Truth be told, sometimes we really don't want to be bothered and really need some rest. A phone call or unexpected visitor is really an intrusion. It is always better to tell the truth and train the children to say, "He is not available right now," rather than lie.

A Sense of Expectation

When the vineyard owner in Jesus' parable came to his vineyard, he came "seeking fruit."[9] He had a desire and a sense of expectation because he *expected* to see fruit on the tree.

Overblown expectations must rank as one of the greatest shocks to young people upon entering the workforce. They waltz into a fast-food restaurant or a department store with visions of large paychecks, free food and merchandise discounts. Then they discover that their boss hired them with different expectations in mind. He expects them to *work* for their pay. That means he expects them to show up on time, to be ready to wash down a kitchen or restroom, to be ready to dice twenty pounds of vegetables or stock five aisles of product before the lunch hour.

I confess that I get irritated when people I hire for a specific job get angry because I have expectations about their performance. Consider me a micromanager if you wish, but when I pay someone to clean the bathrooms in a church building or in my home, I always inspect their work—and I always expect to find a clean bathroom.

God expects us to bear good fruit in our lives. He isn't interested in lip service paid once a week. He inspects our everyday lives to see that we are walking the walk and talking the talk of the kingdom. I am concerned that some Christians have "inherited" the low expectations, laziness and apathy of those who went before them. They resist any effort to help them dream and reach out for something better.

God has a firm answer to that kind of thinking and living. He says, "If any man, woman, boy or girl be in Christ, then they are a new creature. That means that old things, old ways, old sins and old failures have passed away and everything has become new."[10] Regardless of what kind of situation or household you were born into, regardless of what handicap, habit or problem you were born with, once you are *born again* through Jesus

Christ, you have a new mind and a new spirit because you are a new person with a new aim!

God Expects to See Good Fruit in You

The vineyard owner in Luke 13 had expectations of a fruitful year from his fig tree. When it failed to produce for the third year in a row, he gave his vine keeper one more season and said, "If you can't make it produce, cut it down. I'll give it another year, but I expect to see either fruit or another tree in its place."

You and I were saved by God's grace; our works or good deeds had nothing to do with it. After God transplants us into His garden and gives us a fresh start, He expects to see good fruit in our lives as we forget past things and "press toward the goal for the prize."[11]

God is gracious, and He knows that in the beginning of our lives as Christians, things can be difficult as we adjust to a higher standard of conduct. He also knows that good people fall down and fail from time to time. However, He expects each and every one of us to show some progress in due season.

None of us have His permission to stay the way we are. There should be some fruit on the branches of our tree. As we grow and are "cultivated and fertilized" by God's Word and Holy Spirit, He expects to see certain things (sinful ways from the old days) cut off from our lives.

God also expects us to train our children in the same way. If you put something good and holy into your children, then you shouldn't settle for anything less out of them. If they make a mistake, embrace and caress them, but also correct and rebuke them when necessary. Tell them, "You made a mistake. Daddy and Mommy still love you, but we want you to know that we don't expect you to have another baby in this house without being married. We don't expect you to fail another course. We don't expect to see the police bringing you home again. We don't expect you to drop out of high school; we expect you to go to college and own your own home! *We expect it.*"

Under the inspiration of God, David wrote, "He [who delights in God's Word] shall be like a tree planted by the rivers of water, that *brings forth its fruit in its season,* whose leaf also shall not wither; and whatever he does shall prosper."[12]

Now is the season to rebuild your prayer and worship life and to restore the tithe and offerings back into their proper place. Now is the season to take hold of your wayward son and daughter in prayer and in hand and reel them back into God's kingdom.

Seize Your Opportunity to Succeed!

The vine keeper had one more year. This gave him the chance to dig around the fig tree and fertilize it, to prune the branches and examine the roots to pinpoint any problems. The window of opportunity had opened wide; now it was up to him—and the fig tree—to step through the opening and seize the opportunity to succeed.

Some of us are too lazy or fearful to seize the opportunities God sends our way. There are all kinds of college scholarships available, but far too many high school graduates don't go on to college. The opportunity to succeed, the "fourth season," is there for anyone who has the determination to see it through.

It is time for us to seize divine opportunity with the spirit of determination. The Lord is saying to every tree in His vineyard, "I hold My season to account and I'm determined to make this next year count." God has a season for you with your name on it. You were not born to be a failure; you were born with a divine purpose and destiny. Make it bear fruit.

Father, we thank You that we don't have to experience any more wasted seasons in our lives. Because of Your faithfulness, grace and mercy, every season can count for something eternal. We receive the truth and life in Your Word, and we declare by faith that there will be no more wasted seasons. Thank You for giving us another season, another chance. In Jesus' name we pray. Amen.

— **Endnotes** —

[1] Matt. 21:19.

[2] Dan. 2:21.

[3] Gal. 5:22–23.

[4] Prov. 11:30b KJV.

[6] 3 John 2.

[6] I deal primarily with "diseases of the spirit" and how they affect human behavior in this chapter.

[7] Jas. 1:15b KJV.

[8] Jas. 1:13–14.

[9] Luke 13:6.

[10] This is the "Hilliard paraphrase version" of 2 Cor. 5:17.

[11] Phil. 3:13–14.

[12] Ps. 1:3, italics mine.

3

Fear

To the casual observer, it looked like everything was going his way. He was dressed for success, he was trained for fame and everyone who was anyone knew his name. Even his bitter enemies had learned to respect him. This man, Elijah, was God's man of faith and power for the hour. So why would one of the most powerful and feared prophets in the Bible run and hide like a frightened child? The truth is that even mighty men and women of God have not-so-mighty days when their level of faith is low and their expectations for tomorrow are dim.

The story of the prophet Elijah seems to climax in the nineteenth chapter of First Kings.

And Ahab told Jezebel all that Elijah had done, also how he had executed all the prophets with the sword. Then Jezebel sent a messenger to Elijah, saying, "So let the gods do to me, and more also, if I do not make your life as the life of one of them by tomorrow about this

time." And when he saw that, he arose and ran for his life. . . .
(1 Kings 19:1–3, emphasis mine)

Elijah was acting more like a frightened jackrabbit than a
prophet who had just won the most dramatic head-on con-
frontation with evil since Moses had confronted Pharaoh with
God's seven plagues over Egypt and had seen Egypt's finest
drown in the Red Sea. Only one day earlier, Elijah had faced
down and destroyed 450 prophets of Baal in front of all Israel.[1]
Yet something caused him to run for his life after hearing a death
threat from one angry woman. Why?

What Made a Great Prophet Wilt?

One woman's threats sent the prophet running that day, but
he had spent the entire day before taunting, berating and humiliating the pagan priests on King Ahab's payroll. He had boldly
dared hundreds of priests soaked with their own blood to coax a
word out of their deaf and dumb gods of wood and stone; and
then he had heaped aggravation on top of humiliation by soak-
ing the wood of his sacrifice with water before he called upon
God to send fire from heaven to consume it all.[2]

What made one of the greatest prophets in the Bible wilt under
Jezebel's proud boast of revenge? The problem wasn't King Ahab's
Zidonian wife—it was the evil spirit working through her.[3]

When the prophet heard Jezebel's death threat, the first thing
he did was run for the border, to the town of Beersheba in the

territory of Judah. But even that refuge wasn't good enough to calm Elijah's fears; he wanted to put more distance between himself and the woman he feared. So he left his servant in Beersheba and walked alone into the wilderness for a full day. Finally Elijah, the mighty man of God, collapsed under a juniper tree and prayed that God would let him die.

Have you ever felt like just giving up and hiding out? Maybe you felt that way because you were overwhelmed by your situation or the pressures of life. Perhaps you have said to yourself, "If one more issue comes up, if *one more* problem or complaint is dumped in my lap, I am going to pull out my hair—or worse." Elijah had reached the place of total despair: he didn't want to live anymore.

The Bible says that after the prophet prayed, "suddenly an angel touched him, and said to him, 'Arise and eat.'"[4] Elijah ate and drank something and lay down again. Then the angel of the Lord came back a second time, touched him and said, "Arise and eat, because the journey is too great for you."[5] God's provision was so potent that Elijah was able to travel for forty days and nights *on foot* after that angelic meal. God provides what you need for life's journey.

God Meets You at Your Mountain of Desolation

Elijah finally arrived at Mount Horeb, which the Bible calls "the mountain of God." It is interesting to me that the original Hebrew name of this mountain, *Choreb*, means "desolate, parched through drought, to destroy, kill, or decay."[6] Satan is a loudmouthed enemy who is always trying to drive us into a desert region of the soul, hoping we will give up on God and die. You should know, however, that no matter how bad things get in your life, you can count on God's showing up to lift you up. The prophet Elijah found a cave on Mount Horeb and spent the night there. That is when he heard the voice of the Lord say, "What are you doing here, Elijah?"[7]

Do you realize that you serve a God who will back you up even in the bad times? A God who is personally concerned about you and wants to hear about the things that really bother you and deprive you of sleep. You serve a God who wants to step into your neighborhood, walk down your street and up your pathway, walk through the front door and up your stairs, and ring your doorbell until you open the door and let Him in.

When He asks you what you are doing, you don't have to put on airs with Him. You don't have to whitewash the facts, to make things look a certain way. This is the God whose Son died on a rugged cross for you, and He is concerned about the rough, rugged and raw parts of our lives too.

If You Lose Heaven's Perspective, You Will Lose Your Way

When Elijah heard God's question, he couldn't contain his emotions. He launched into a long complaint about his situation that ended with the words, "I alone am left; and they seek to take my life."[8] At this point, even Elijah the great prophet had fallen into the trap of spiritual nearsightedness that all of us encounter from time to time. He had taken his eyes off of God and put them on himself and his problems. First he lost his heavenly perspective, and then he lost his way altogether. But God was about to correct Elijah's problem.

Elijah had to understand that he was not alone. When we become so overcome by personal pressures that we go into a "cave" of seclusion to hide from our problems, we lose sight of the fact that we are really not alone in the world. Elijah responded to God's question by saying, "I've tried to do Your will, God. I tried to slay the false prophets, but now I am all alone. I'm the only one who is still alive and faithful to You. What can I do?"[9] Notice how God responded to Elijah.

First He assigned him helpers—he told him to seek out Hazael, Jehu and Elisha and anoint them to execute God's will against His enemies.[10] Then He said, "Yet I have reserved seven thousand in Israel, all whose knees have not bowed to Baal, and every mouth that has not kissed him."[11]

Elijah had to get some perspective so he could hear what God was saying. When you are in an isolated cave of hurt and self-pity, you tend to cut yourself off from other people and even your support system. When you allow your problems and fears to isolate you, you can become so depressed that you will do everything but the right thing. If you hear what God is trying to say to you in the midst of sorrow and suffering, He will use it to turn your situation around and bless you.

The Devil's Bark Is Stronger Than His Bite

You may not be facing death threats, but you do have an enemy who wants you dead—or the same as dead. The Bible says, "Be sober, be vigilant; because your adversary the devil walks about like a roaring lion, seeking whom he may devour."[12]

Notice that the Bible says he struts around *like* he is a lion, but he isn't. The devil's bark is always stronger than his bite. He is like a chained beast with only a limited area of authority. He is a created being, not the Creator. Furthermore, he is a totally *defeated* devil, with no true power or authority over the saints of God.

In your encounters and battles with this fallen prince, you should remember four simple things we see in Elijah's life. I call them the "Four Ds." The first three words describe commendable traits in Elijah's life that should be in the lives of every disciple of Christ. The fourth trait is a human trait. Knowing about it helps us to deal with it when it surfaces in our own lives and ministries.

1. Elijah was *devoted* to God. He had a prayer life, he had a relationship with God and God spoke to him. However, Elijah's devotion to God did not insulate him from life's problems. God does not promise a life without challenges. Indeed, the Bible promises us that "all who desire to live godly in Christ Jesus will suffer persecution."[13] You will experience disappointments and tribulation in this world,

and sometimes you will be hurt and feel frustrated by the things people say and do. You may even be tempted to be aggravated with God because He didn't do what you thought He should do.

Someone once told me, "Pray for me; I've lost a loved one. I love God, but I'm angry and irritated with Him too. I'm just like a shell—something inside me has died and I don't understand why. I've been devoted to God, I've been a prayer warrior, I've fasted, I've lifted my hands and paid my tithes, and I bring my offerings faithfully." I told this young woman, "Just because you were devoted to God does not mean that you will never go through trouble. It means that when trouble comes, you will get through it." Trouble will come but it will not defeat you.

2. Elijah was *dutiful* to obey God, even when that obedience put him at risk. It was no small thing to confront the king of his nation with his sin when, according to the custom of the day, the king had the power of life and death over every citizen of Israel. Yet God told Elijah to confront King Ahab and tell him there would be no rain in Israel until he spoke the word at God's command.

3. Elijah's devotion to God and dutiful obedience qualified and equipped him to *destroy* the works of the devil and the enemies of God. John defined Jesus' mission this way: "For this purpose the Son of God was manifested, that He might destroy the works of the devil."[14] We have the same calling today in His name and authority. We must destroy

everything that is false in our lives. That includes the false gods of consumerism, false relationships, false loyalties (to our television sets, our pop heroes and our bank accounts) and every false image of God that robs us of time we should devote to the one true God who has made for us "a way out of no way."

4. I especially want to focus on the fourth point: Elijah's human trait called *depression*. This prophet was devoted to God and was dutiful to obey and destroy the false gods that had polluted Israel. He did what God told him to do, the way he was told to do it and in the time frame God gave him. Yet just after the moment of total victory in the face of impossible odds, this man of God fell into a state of utter depression.

From Glory to the Wilderness

Even Jesus was acquainted with the ups and downs of life on earth. If you look closely at the Gospels, you will notice that immediately after the high point in Jesus' life when John the Baptist baptized the Lord in the River Jordan and the Holy Spirit descended upon Him—moments after God the Father's voice thundered from heaven, "This is My beloved Son, in whom I am well pleased"—something impossibly odd happened. In both the Gospel of Matthew and the Gospel of Luke, the very next sentence describes how the Holy Spirit led Jesus into the wilderness where He was tempted by the devil![15]

It is not uncommon for the high moments in our lives to be followed by a plunge into personal depression. Many authors say they feel terribly depressed after they complete a great book. I experienced this "roller-coaster effect" in my own life after completing a massive building project at the Cathedral International, where I serve as senior pastor and bishop.

I had been asked to speak at the Martin Luther King Jr. Chapel at Morehouse College one week before we were to have the grand opening for our cathedral. I was standing there in that august chapel wearing my doctoral robe and feeling quite good—or so I thought. I began to speak and was trying to stick closely to my notes. I reached page four when I suddenly turned as white as my robe. I am told that I collapsed to the floor, but all I can remember is hearing a nurse who came to the stage from the congregation say, "I'm not getting a reading."

I was just conscious enough to think, *Am I dead?* My wife was with me on that trip, although she generally stays home to care for our young children. I like to joke that she jumped up to the stage and took my hand to ask earnestly, "Is the insurance signed over?" The truth is that she held my hand while I seriously wondered if I was going to leave this realm for good.

What happened? I had gone too far, and my body rebelled. The months I'd spent overseeing the design, construction and financing of our large building project had taken their toll. After our final moment of great relief and accomplishment, I fell victim to a time of personal sickness. I didn't want to admit it, but my body made it clear that I was physically depleted and emotionally drained. And even though I had enjoyed all the wonderful celebrations, the ribbon cuttings and the dedicatory services and prayers, I was depressed.

All too often, those who are responsible for feeding the flock of God fail to find spiritual food and refreshment for themselves. The leaders who are responsible for leading God's people in worship often fail to understand the importance of being worshippers themselves in times when they have only an audience of One—God Himself.

If you think about it, it is common for hair stylists to have second-rate coiffures because they are too busy doing everyone else's hair to properly care for their own. People who cook for a living are often malnourished. Why? After they slice the roast beef, bone the chicken and bake the potatoes, in their haste they will snack on a biscuit or one of the desserts. By the time they have the opportunity to eat the meal they've prepared, they don't have an appetite. And so it is with preachers.

Only Flesh and Blood

Paul the apostle wrote, "But we have this treasure in earthen vessels, that the excellence of the power may be of God and not of us."[16] I don't care how anointed you may be; you are still only flesh and blood. That means you are still prone to getting angry, depressed, annoyed, irritable and generally acting like a heathen once in a while. That doesn't mean you are not sanctified or that you don't love God. It simply means that God's treasure is packed inside your earthen vessel, a container with known limitations. God knows that His earthen vessels occasionally need to hear someone say, "I'm standing with you."

The apostle Paul outlined the differences between feeling extreme pressure and succumbing to defeat when you feel like giving up and hiding out. He said, in his second letter to the Corinthians:

> *We are hard pressed on every side, yet not crushed; we are perplexed, but not in despair; persecuted, but not forsaken; struck down, but not destroyed—always carrying about in the body the dying of the Lord Jesus, that the life of Jesus also may be manifested in our body. (2 Cor. 4:8–10)*

If you are breathing, then you probably know how it feels to be "hard pressed on every side." Everywhere you turn there is a problem to face or a challenge ready to bring pressure into your life. If you don't have a problem in your marriage, then problems will surface with your children or your job. If those areas are prospering, you may see a challenge rise up in your relationships at church. Everyone has pressures in their lives—young, old, black, white, male, female, employed, unemployed. The key to success is learning how to shift the weight of life's burdens on to the broad shoulders of Jesus so those pressures do not lead to your undoing. The Bible says you must cast "all your care upon Him, for He cares for you."[17]

There are no perfect people in God's kingdom—just a perfect

Savior who extends to us perfect grace to cover our perfectly normal shortcomings. When you are troubled on every side, the best thing you can do is be still and know that He is still God.[18]

Finish with Boldness

The apostle Paul knew what it was like to be hard pressed on every side, yet he ended with a bold disclaimer: "Yet we are not crushed." This is the right reaction to pure in-your-face trouble.

Uncertainty is another source of pressure that produces stress. The apostle wrote, "We are perplexed, but not in despair." Any seasoned leader will quickly admit that there are many times in a life or ministry when he or she is perplexed. Maturity and past experience with the faithfulness of God can help us to avoid despair in those "seeking" times.

In this passage, Paul describes two of the most difficult pressures any Christian will face in this life, pressures encountered by Jesus Himself: we are *"persecuted,* but not *forsaken; struck down,* but not *destroyed."*

Elijah's flight from Jezebel helps us understand what Paul was saying to the Corinthians. The Bible says, "And there [Elijah] went into a cave, and spent the night in that place; and behold, the word of the LORD came to him."[19] The pressure of life had made this great prophet run and hide from everything and everyone—except for God. Immersed in depression and overcome with frustration, Elijah had reached the lowest point anyone can: he wanted to die and get it over with.

Unchecked depression and unrestrained pressures can cause you to hide in a cave of isolation or to become involved in bad relationships. Sometimes in the depths of depression lonely people begin to think to themselves, *Anyone would be better than no one.* My wife and I have ministered to many Christian men and women who fell into this state of mind when their frustration and loneliness finally overcame their better judgment. In their pain, they reasoned to themselves, *Well, half a man (or half a woman) is better than no man (or no woman).* I've seen a number of women settle for "half of a man"—someone who was going to "smack them in the morning, beat them at lunchtime and then try to get romantic after dinner." It is always better to wait upon God to send you His best instead of rushing ahead to settle for second-best. The lonely season of the cave is just that— it is a season. Remember the words, "this, too, shall pass."

You may be sad today, but you will be glad tomorrow. You may be mourning today, but you will be dancing tomorrow. You may not have a job today, but God will open the door to one tomorrow. Every new day brings a new opportunity for a miracle. Every tomorrow is filled with the promises of God, and the promises of God are "yea and amen."[20]

We need to understand that, as Elijah experienced, the pressures that make us want to run and hide are not just spiritual in nature—*there are physical factors to be considered as well.* God knew that His prophet was physically exhausted, famished and dangerously dehydrated. That is why He sent an angel to meet him with provisions for his physical needs. I believe that this also explains why God pointed Elijah toward a cave on Mount Horeb; He knew the man needed to sleep before he could listen.

Sometimes wisdom requires us to gently tell our children, "Honey, it's not you. Daddy is just tired. Mommy is just hungry. Give us a little time to rest and eat something, and then we'll be ready to go outside with you and play."

At other times, you need *more* than food, drink and sleep. You need an encounter with the living God. You need to hear the voice of your Maker confirming your worth and reestablishing your purpose for living. Elijah needed to hear from God, and he did; but even this event was a learning process for the prophet— as it can be for us.

A Very Human Response

After Elijah had had a good night's sleep, God gave him a wake-up call. The Lord asked Elijah why he was hiding in a cave, and the prophet responded just the way we would. He complained that he was the last faithful saint left standing in Israel. Then it was God's turn to respond.

First, the Lord changed the location of their conversation. He knew Elijah needed a change of scenery. Darkness and isolation were of no value for the depressed prophet at this stage. So God commanded him to step outside the cave and stand on the mountain before Him.[21]

The Bible tells us that the Lord simply passed by Elijah's location and that it was battered by a wind powerful enough to shatter rock formations on the mountain. That phenomenon was followed by an earthquake, and then by a fire. Yet God's *voice* wasn't in any of these spectacular occurrences.

The Scriptures imply that Elijah didn't bother to obey God's command during these dramatic displays. It was when the prophet heard the "still small voice" of God that he wrapped his face in his mantle and *moved* to stand in the entrance to the cave. Sometimes God is not moving in the shouting or the noise of a happy crowd. Sometimes God moves in a whisper, in the midst of a quiet prayer.

My friend, you need to take the time to be still and quiet long enough to hear the voice of God. The wisest course is to pray, "Lord, please speak. If You want to speak through the earthquake, then speak and I will listen. If You want to speak through the fire, then speak and I will listen. But when You want to speak through a still small voice, help me quiet myself long enough to hear what You have to say to me."

Once God had coaxed Elijah out of his cave of depression, He quickly helped him adjust his "poor me" attitude and gave him vital answers to his heart's cry. "You say you are alone?" God said, "You are not alone. I've got seven thousand others who haven't bowed their knee and never will." Then he proceeded to give Elijah some practical, strategic advice. "I want you to contact three people to help you finish your work in Israel. Anoint Hazael as the new king of Syria (he will be your ally instead of your enemy); anoint Jehu as king over Israel (don't worry about Ahab; he's history); and anoint Elisha as prophet in your place."[22]

Too Prophetic to Live Pathetic

The Bible doesn't say this, but I think God must have said quietly to Himself, "When their training is complete, Elijah, you are coming home with Me."

God is saying to all of us, "It is time to come out of your cave of sorrow. Leave your hidden hole of self-pity, depression and self-accusation behind. I care about you and am concerned about your future. I will bring you out."

Elijah was too prophetic to live pathetic—and so are you.

The Lord told his weary prophet, "Listen, you've been feeling sorry for yourself long enough. It is time to get up and be delivered. It is time for you to get up and go back to work." And once God had brought him through, Elijah never again returned to the cave of desolation. You may have been depressed yesterday, and you probably felt like giving up and giving in. Perhaps you were sure last night that all your friends had deserted you; maybe you even contemplated taking your own life. But today is a whole new day. God is speaking to you, and there is no need to run and hide anymore.

If you are still hiding in a cave of desolation, isolation and frustration, I have a word from the Lord for you: It is time to come out of your cave and step out into your destiny in Christ.

— Endnotes

1. 1 Kings 18:20–40.

2. 1 Kings 18:27–28, 33–35, 38–40.

3. That "Jezebel spirit" still roams through our churches and cities today, causing many men and women of God to follow in Elijah's frightened footsteps as they run from their pastoral responsibilities in fear for their lives and sanity.

4. 1 Kings 19:5.

5. 1 Kings 19:7.

6. James Strong, *Strong's Exhaustive Concordance of the Bible* (Peabody, MA: Hendrickson Publishers, n.d.); meanings and definitions drawn from the word derivations for **Horeb** (Hebrew, #2722, 2717).

7. 1 Kings 19:9b.

8. 1 Kings 19:10b.

9. This is my paraphrase of 1 Kings 19:14.

10. 1 Kings 19:15–17.

11. 1 Kings 19:18.

12. 1 Pet. 5:8.

13. 2 Tim. 3:12.

14. 1 John 3:8b.

15. Matt. 4:1; Luke 4:1.

16. 2 Cor. 4:7.

17. 1 Pet. 5:7.

18. Ps. 46:10.

19. 1 Kings 19:9.

20. 2 Cor. 1:20 KJV.

21. 1 Kings 19:11.

22. 1 Kings 19:15–18, according to the "Hilliard paraphrase version."

4

Failure

We don't like to talk about failure. I can count on one hand the times I have preached on failure. When I publicly state that failure is a part of the Christian journey, I can be sure that one of the "deeper Christians" around will reply, "No, it's not. The Christian life is about victory." But you gain victory only when you learn how to rise above failures and overcome them.

God can use the "closed door" of our failure to change our direction and usher us through His open door. He can carefully steer us through our journey of failure and success, all the while moving us toward the center of His purposes so we can be what we were called to be. No one typifies this process more than the disciple who failed.

The Gospel of Matthew tells us that on the night He was betrayed, Jesus took His disciples to the mount of Olives and told them, "All ye shall be offended because of me this night: for it is written, I will smite the shepherd, and the sheep of the flock shall be scattered abroad."[1]

The Greek word that has been translated as "offended" in the King James Version is *skandalizo*. It means exactly what it sounds like in the English language. Jesus warned the disciples that they were going to be "scandalized, entrapped, and tripped up"; they were going to "stumble and be enticed to sin" because of Him.[2]

What happened next has, in an odd way, brought untold comfort to millions of Christians for nearly two thousand years. Peter, the most impetuous, loudmouthed, brash and uncouth member of the team, once again stepped forward to say his piece. Every born-again human being who admits to having flaws or imperfections should lean forward in anticipation every time Peter's story is told. For this saint of the common man probably boasted to Jesus in all sincerity: "Though *all men* shall be offended because of thee, yet will *I* never be offended."[3]

Jesus answered Peter's claim to special virtue with the prophecy that Peter would betray Him three times before sunrise. Dismayed by the Master's lack of faith in him, Peter stubbornly decided to stick with his boast, and he even expanded it a little for good measure: "Though I should die with thee, yet will I not deny thee."[4] Then all the other disciples followed Peter's lead and made the same boast.

Moments later Jesus took the disciples with him to Gethsemane, where Peter and the others failed to spend even one hour in prayer with the Master in His darkest hour.[5] Jesus woke Peter up and warned him to watch and pray so he wouldn't fall into temptation: "The spirit indeed is willing but the flesh is weak,"[6] He said. When the Lord came back a second time, Peter and the other disciples were again sleeping, so He returned alone to His place of agonized prayer.

Before dawn's light, Jesus had submitted Himself to the betrayer's kiss and the armed guards dispatched by the high priest. As for His "loyal" disciples, they had slipped away into the darkness of the night—even Peter. It is critical to understand the effects of pressure and how it can lead even the most boastful person to slip away. Handling life's pressure can become burdensome and overwhelming when we are not willing to analyze our own impoverished moral condition.

Some of us have made such a mess of our lives and betrayed the Lord so often that we wonder why God would want to bother with us at all. Frankly, we are embarrassed at how little it really takes for us to temporarily betray the things of God. We have made terrible decisions out of fear and frustration. We have acted like cowards when we should have acted with courage. We have stood by silently when we should have boldly spoken up on behalf of Christ or His kingdom.

It is not that we do not love God, for we do. For the most part, we walk with God every day. But it is in the moment of testing and trial, or when we meet a certain kind of person or find ourselves in a certain mood, that we fail. Certain seasons of the soul, certain days and certain pressures in our lives cause us to follow in proud Peter's footsteps, and we miserably fail our Lord.

Our journey in faith begins when we receive Christ as our Savior, but it is just that—a *beginning*. Most of us were baptized in water to publicly seal our transformation from darkness to light with a physical act. Thus we begin the lifelong journey as those who are marked out and set aside as holy children of God toward "sanctification," or separation from the ways of darkness.

When we decide to follow the Lord, we are instantly changed in our spirit, but our thinking and our learned behaviors are slow and stubbornly reluctant to change; yet change we do. We begin by crawling; we learn more about the new life in Christ by taking in God's Word in tiny increments, like infants receiving a mother's milk. In time, the outward transformation of the mind and body begins to accelerate as we come of age and consume God's Word, just as growing young adults eat adult portions of solid foods.[7]

Finding Hope

I don't mean to belittle the pain Peter's failure caused, but I'm glad there was a disciple who failed. Peter's failure when he was under intense pressure, and his subsequent success, give me hope and encouragement that there is hope for me too.

The truth is that *all of us* have stumbled and tripped more times than we want people to know. This explains why most of us are intensely interested in Peter's story. "What happened to Peter after that? Tell us, did he get a second chance? Tell me the story again—did Jesus *really* forgive Peter?"

Sometimes we go to church and have a glorious time in God's presence. But by the time we reach the parking lot, all the anointing has leaked out. Someone rubbed us the wrong way or said something that aggravated our nerves, and "all that glory leaked out."

It is amazing how many of us have holes in our spirit.[8] You and I have a personal relationship with God. The good news is that victory in the Christian life often involves getting up after a failure.

Peter was determined to get up from his fallen state and find his way back to God no matter what it cost. There are four crucial facts about Peter that we need to recognize so we can learn and live in victory despite our many failures.

Fact 1: Peter Was a Disciple

A disciple is a disciplined one, a follower. Whether we like it or not, Jesus has given us only one road to choose if we want to follow Him: "If any man will come after me, let him deny himself, and take up his cross daily, and follow me."[9]

Although a total of twelve disciples occupied center stage with Jesus Christ in the Gospels, Jesus invited three of them to accompany Him to the "mount of transfiguration" where He revealed His glory. They were Peter, James and John.

Peter was a true disciple who had exhibited tremendous spiritual discernment at times. He was the first of the twelve to recognize Jesus as the Christ, the Anointed One of God.[10] Yet almost in the same breath, Peter had managed to put his foot in his mouth and earn perhaps the severest rebuke Jesus uttered in the New Testament, when Jesus told him, "Get behind Me, Satan! You are an offense [*skandalon*] to Me, for you are not mindful of the things of God, but the things of men."[11] (Sometimes I think that chronic foot-in-mouth disease is one of the prerequisites to being a human.)

The clearest description of how the Lord looks at human failure is found in His instruction to—you guessed it—Peter, on the night he boasted that he would stand fast with Jesus even though everybody else might run away:

> And the Lord said, "Simon, Simon! Indeed, Satan has asked for you, that he may sift you as wheat. But I have prayed for you, that your faith should not fail; and when you have returned to Me, strengthen your brethren." (Luke 22:31–32)

Jesus was telling the disciple who would soon fail Him miserably, "I prayed for you *that your faith will not fail, even when your testimony does.*" Satan has desired to have *you* too, so he can sift you, shake you up, unsettle and disintegrate your effectiveness. Much in the same way, the pressures of life, when unchecked, can place a stranglehold on the most free-thinking, optimistic person in any given situation. Pressure, when mismanaged, can break you.

This is Satan's desire. Your Adversary wants you to be impotent in your walk with Christ so that you can be reduced to nothing more than a lifeless piece in a museum, a static picture, a still image preserved from the vibrant life that once was. You need to know that because you are His disciple; the Bible says Jesus is at the right hand of the Father interceding for you.[12]

I am sad to say there are many churches in this land that have been sifted too. They have their Hammond B-3s and thundering pipe organs set in position, and their musicians are in place. All their wonderfully padded pews are lined up in flawless rows, under the kaleidoscopic light streaming from their exquisite stained-glass windows.

The only problem is that one item didn't pass through the sifting process, because hearts changed along the way, and the power of God is void because the church has been sifted and their faith failed the test.[13] Individual believers and churches alike need to learn from Peter's example.

Jesus' prophecy about Peter came true within a matter of hours, but Peter had some lifelong habits that contributed to his failure. For one thing, Peter had a habit of speaking when he should have been listening. In biblical terms, Peter's habit was the opposite of God's ideal: He was quick to speak and slow to hear; and he was also quick to grow angry.[14] He should have been listening carefully that night at the Last Supper, but instead he tried to outtalk Jesus.

The Lord tried to warn Peter about this danger, but He couldn't tell him much. Peter was a professional fisherman, rough, rugged and raw. He knew how to tie knots in nets or lines, how to maneuver boats in a high wind and how to pull in overloaded fishing nets in a high sea. Outwardly, I believe he was a man's man— very masculine and action-oriented. Not much of a listener.

Unfortunately, one of the drawbacks of being that kind of man is that most of the time other people can't tell you anything. This listening problem afflicts Christians of both genders. Peter exemplifies many Christians today who are so thickheaded that they can't receive advice or good counsel from anyone.

Peter was so sure he was different from everybody else. I can almost hear him say, "Lord, I've been with You three whole years now. Do You remember the day You healed my mother-in-law? How about the time we raised Jairus's daughter? Do You remember how I was full of faith? Then there was the time we fed five thousand men with only two scrawny fish and five loaves of bread! We go way back, don't we, Lord? Trust me on this: Everybody else may cut and run, but not me. I don't care what You go through—You can count on me. Even if I have to die for You, you can count me in to the end."

Another reason Peter failed is because he was sleeping when he should have been watching and praying. Peter didn't *listen* to the Lord's warning at the supper table about how Satan wanted to break him. He also wasn't listening to, or else he purposely ignored, Jesus when He told Peter to "watch and pray" to avoid falling into temptation. The result was inevitable.

Your spirit can have power over your flesh—*if you feed it.* What would Peter have done when he was tempted to deny Jesus if he had been praying instead of sleeping that night? Any disciple who wants to maintain a disciplined walk with the Lord must know how to be slow to speak and quick to pray.

But even when we fail, all is not lost. God's Word has a

wonderful promise for any disciple who fails. Paul wrote to the church at Corinth:

> *Therefore let him who thinks he stands take heed lest he fall. No temptation has overtaken you except such as is common to man; but God is faithful, who will not allow you to be tempted beyond what you are able, but with the temptation will also make the way of escape, that you may be able to bear it. (1 Cor. 10:12–13)*

God's Word promises you that every situation that confronts you and presses you up against the wall of failure and ruin is *not* a dead end. Because of Christ, there is always a way of escape from ruin and collapse. The real problem comes when we choose not to walk through God's open door of escape.

This much you can count on: There is a test coming with your name on it, whether you are ready or not. Peter fell into sin because he was so full of himself at a time when he should have been focusing on every word that came from the Lord's lips. In God's kingdom, humility is the winning attitude, not arrogant boasting and presumptuous proclamations. The disciple who failed later wrote an apostolic letter to the churches under his care, saying, "Humble yourselves therefore under the mighty hand of God, that he may exalt you in due time."[15] Humility is a virtue that true disciples can't afford to do without. When we get to the place where no one can tell us anything, we are preparing for failure.

Fact 2: Peter Allowed Himself to Become Distanced from Jesus (and His Brethren)

Peter distanced himself from his brethren when he claimed he would pass the test even if everybody else failed. Even if such a claim were true, only God gets the glory for any ability to stand in trials and tribulations. Then came the moment of truth for Peter, when Judas Iscariot and the temple guards led Jesus away:

> *Then took they him, and led him, and brought him into the high priest's house. And* Peter followed afar off. *And when they had kindled a fire in the midst of the hall, and were set down together,* Peter sat down among them. *(Luke 22:54–55, emphasis mine)*

This passage contains a threefold recipe for denying the One who brought us out of darkness:

Number one, Peter followed Jesus from "afar off," or from a *distance.*

Number two, he went so far as to sit down among the very people who were persecuting his Lord!

Number three, Peter chose to heat himself by the wrong fire.

Genuine Christians don't wake up one morning and make a decision to deny their Lord. Denial comes through a slow, progressive process, in such small incremental steps that you are almost unaware of how far you have slipped away from the truth. But if you mix these three ingredients of the recipe for denial, it will cause certain spiritual death!

Peter's problems began when he made a loud, proud boast instead of confessing his weakness and drawing close to God. His problem quickly spiraled out of control once he started following Jesus *from a distance.*

When you follow the Lord at a distance, too much can come between you. We began our journey of life *close to the altar* where our redemption was won and received. Honestly, the safest position in the world is the place of being bound to the altar, the place of sacrifice.

The truth is that with every step you take away from God, the cross of Christ grows smaller, more distant and more insignificant in your life. Sooner or later, you won't even look back to see if you are still with Him. Some of us put so much distance between our daily lives and our life that we begin to toy with the edge of darkness. Eventually we will come so precariously close to the edge that we may fall. The same thing happens in our interpersonal relationships, with marriage partners, family members, friends and people in the local church.

Peter followed the Lord from afar, and he stopped feeling enough passion for Jesus to overcome his fear of man. When you follow the Lord from afar, you can miss church and skip prayer without it bothering you. Something is wrong here, because personal and corporate prayer, worship and fellowship in the church become second nature for Christians.

The disciple who failed his Master sat down with His accusers when they made a fire. He warmed himself by a hostile fire just a few yards away from where Jesus was being beaten mercilessly by His captors. Peter was sitting there looking in, but he wasn't going in. His proud boast was quickly forgotten in the moment of crisis.

Fact 3: Peter Denied the Lord

Peter made his first denial of his Savior when a lowly slave girl looked closely at him and said, "This man was also with Him."[16] Peter quickly answered in a tone that implies he was putting his accuser in her place, "Woman, I know him not."[17]

The second denial came shortly after the first. It happened that "another," possibly a male servant attached to the high priest's household, looked closely at Peter and said, "You also are of them."[18] Peter's answer was hot and instant: the cross of martyrdom was getting too close for his comfort: "Man, I am not!"[19]

Peter's third and most searing denial of Jesus came when a third accuser pointed at Peter with the same bold confidence Peter had exhibited the night before. He said, "Surely this fellow also was with Him, for *he is a Galilean*,"[20] something that was obvious because of his accent.[21] Peter felt cornered when faced with such a confident and persistent accuser who had singled him out from the crowd.

The word *Galilee* comes from a Hebrew word that means "the heathen circle."[22] Jews who came from that region were ranked just above Gentiles or "dogs," and their distinctive accents, clothing and customs often set them apart from other Jews. Therefore, being recognized as a Galilean made Peter incredibly uncomfortable. (Christians in our day still have a low tolerance for being set apart from the crowd.) Then Peter decided to distance himself even further from Jesus by doing what would normally be unthinkable: "He began to curse and swear, saying, 'I do not know the Man!' And immediately a rooster crowed,"[23] and Jesus' word came back to haunt Peter.

The key to standing with Jesus is staying close to Him. We do that by praying fervently, often, honestly and long. Even if you don't say a word, get in His presence. Most of the time we dismiss a problem someone else has by telling ourselves, "I would never do that." That sounds strangely familiar, doesn't it? Our denials usually aren't as dramatic or costly as Peter's, but they are just as wrong.

You deny Him when you shrink back from witnessing to the strangers, friends or coworkers you meet every day, fearing their rejection. You deny Him when you hear people ripping apart your church or the Lord in conversation—*but remain silent* like Peter, warming your hands around a hostile fire.

The Church of Jesus Christ is the same church that visited you when you were in the hospital and gave you money so you would keep your lights on. This is the body of believers that helped you get back home after your mother died. These are the people who gave you a basket of food at Thanksgiving, and they belong to the same Lord who saved you from sin, shame and degradation. This is the same church that kept you from losing your mind; these are the blood-washed people who walked down that dark path with you when you buried your loved one.

If you and I really identify with Jesus, if we really love Him, then we must be willing to step in harm's way for the sake of the cross every day of our lives. This is much easier said than done, but we are not in this alone. We have been given a Comforter, a Guide and a Teacher in God the Holy Spirit. When you fall—and you will—He is there to pick you up.

Peter sincerely hoped to follow a Messiah whose kingdom did not involve a cross. That is why he stuck his foot in his mouth by trying to "correct" Jesus Christ for saying He was destined to die on that rugged tree.[24] But he soon discovered that the cross was the crux of our deliverance, the signpost of our divine destiny in Christ. You cannot follow Jesus without becoming intimately acquainted with a cross of your own.[25] If we would share His glory and His resurrection, we must also share in His suffering.[26]

Fact 4: Peter Was Distraught

Peter's faith ran him right back to the altar of true repentance before God. The Bible tells us Peter instantly knew he had sinned; he promptly forgot about the people around him and rushed out into the darkness where he *wept bitterly.* This is what the Bible calls "godly sorrow."[27]

The only proper response for a Christian who has denied the Lord is brokenhearted repentance. The very fact that you feel godly sorrow for your sin is an irrefutable sign that you are a child of God and a disciple of Jesus Christ.

Peter lost his testimony, but he didn't lose his faith. His faith drew him right back to the Lord, and he soon discovered just how deep God's mercy, grace and love can be. When it was first learned that the Lord's grave was empty, the angels at the entrance said, "But go your way, tell his disciples *and Peter.*"[28]

There are thousands of "Peters" hiding in their homes at this moment because they failed. They are so embarrassed by their failure that they have begun to follow Jesus from a distance; they have separated themselves from the brethren and the Church. We have the responsibility to take the Master's urgent message to Peter, wherever he may be found in our generation: It is time to come back home. The Master is waiting for you. The truth is that we, too, have failed God. Not only are we saved "by grace," but *it is by grace that we serve, suffer, survive and overcome!*

We have wept bitterly over our fall and our failures, and now it is time for every Peter in Christ's family to come back home. Peter, it's time to come back home and get back in the choir once again. There is a place for you on the usher board, and, Peter, you need to step back into the vital service of worship to the King. Your voice is needed, your hands are missed, your presence is precious and Jesus wants to meet you at the altar of your sorrow. I know you failed, but Jesus told me to go get you, Peter:

You don't have to lose your faith
because you've temporarily lost your testimony.

Peter denied the Lord, but his faith in the Lord led him to true repentance and genuine restoration. The power of God makes even our mistakes, our failures and our stumbling work together for good.[29]

The disciple who failed was the same person who boldly stood up in front of thousands of devout Jews on a high holy day and preached the first sermon under the New Covenant! He was so powerful and anointed that three thousand Jews received Jesus Christ as Messiah as a result of his uncompromising witness to the resurrection![30]

The same disciple who once ran away from a young maid in fear didn't bother to ask the audience of thousands of Jews to receive Jesus that day. He *demanded* it. He said, *"Repent, and be baptized every one of you* in the name of Jesus Christ for the remission of sins, and ye shall receive the gift of the Holy Ghost."[31]

The disciple who denied Christ three times because of fear now began to preach and proclaim with the same boldness of His Master when he shouted to thousands of Jewish people gathered in Jerusalem itself, "Be saved from this perverse generation."[32]

Is your name Peter? Are you the disciple who failed?
It is time to come home.
The Lord told me to seek you out.

— Endnotes —

1 Matt. 26:31 KJV.

2 James Strong, *Strong's Exhaustive Concordance of the Bible* (Peabody, MA: Hendrickson Publishers, n.d.); **offended** (Greek, #4624, 4625).

3 Matt. 26:33 KJV, emphasis mine.

4 Matt. 26:35 KJV.

5 Matt. 26:40–41.

6 Matt. 26:41.

7 1 Cor. 3:2; Heb. 5:12.

8 No, I am *not* trying to come up with a new doctrine or theological concept. I am merely trying to express in everyday language what happens when God's "new wine" is poured into an old, unrepaired wineskin.

9 Luke 9:23 KJV.

10 Matt. 16:16; Mark 8:29; John 6:69.

11 Matt. 16:23.

12 Indeed, for all the saints. Rom. 8:34.

13 2 Tim. 3:5; 1 Cor. 4:20.

14 Jas. 1:19.

15 1 Pet. 5:6 KJV.

16 Luke 22:56b.

17 Luke 22:57 KJV.

18 Luke 22:58b.

19 Ibid.

20 Luke 22:59b, emphasis mine.

21 Matt. 26:73.

22 Strong, *Strong's Exhaustive Concordance of the Bible;* **Galilee, Galilean** (Greek, #1057, 1056; Hebrew, #1551).

[23] Matt 26:74.

[24] Matt. 16:22.

[25] Luke 9:23.

[26] 1 Pet. 2:21.

[27] 2 Cor. 7:10 says, "For godly sorrow produces repentance leading to salvation, not to be regretted; but the sorrow of the world produces death."

[28] Mark 16:7 KJV, italics mine.

[29] Rom. 8:28.

[30] Acts 2:41.

[31] Acts 2:38 KJV, italics mine.

[32] Acts 2:40b.

5

Self-Deception

The literature of every age is filled with warnings about the dangers, weaknesses, appetites and sins hidden within the human soul and body. You can find them in the pages of history, in classic Greek tales, in medical metaphors and in the eternal wisdom of the Bible.

The list is virtually endless: "beauty is only skin-deep"; Trojan Horse; "the cancer within"; "beautiful without and rotten to the core"; the Achilles' heel; "ye shall know them by their fruits"; "a chain is only as strong as its weakest link"; "out of the abundance of the heart the mouth speaks" and more.

Is it possible the apostle Paul had in mind these enemies within when he wrote his first letter to the spiritually immature church at Corinth? At one point, he described the historic error of the Israelites in the Old Testament and wrote, "But with most of them God was not well pleased, for their bodies were scattered in the wilderness. *Now these things became our examples. . . .*"[1]

The Israelites experienced the glory of God dwelling among them. They saw great miracles happen in front of their eyes, and they came to be known as the people of God. So how did these people go from such a place of divine blessing, protection and favor to making God so angry that He allowed every one of them who was twenty years old and older to die in the wilderness?

They became overconfident and overfamiliar with the presence of God. Soon they began to lack the self-discipline they needed to continue living in God's favor. Self-discipline is one of the keys to success in life.

God declared, "My people are destroyed for lack of knowledge."[2] We need godly knowledge so that we can overcome and not be destroyed. The *example* of the generation of Israelites under the leadership of Moses in the desert reveals **five significant sins** that led to their destruction:

1. The Israelites *refused to yield to the move of God.* The Israelites grumbled and resisted Moses' authority from the Red Sea to the River Jordan, and when it came time to cross the river, they wanted to stone God's messengers and faithful "spies" because they had the truth.[3]

2. They were *unfaithful to God.* Even as Moses was receiving the Ten Commandments that would mark them as God's chosen people for generations to come, they were pressuring Aaron to make them a golden calf. Then they began to worship and rejoice before this pagan image, made by man's hands.

READER/CUSTOMER CARE SURVEY

We care about your opinions. Please take a moment to fill out this Reader Survey card and mail it back to us.
As a special **"thank you"** we'll send you exciting news about interesting books and a valuable **Gift Certificate.**

Please PRINT using ALL CAPS

First Name [＿＿＿＿＿＿＿＿＿＿] MI. [＿] Last Name [＿＿＿＿＿＿＿＿＿＿]

Address [＿＿＿＿＿＿＿＿＿＿＿＿＿＿＿＿＿＿＿＿＿]

City [＿＿＿＿＿＿＿＿] ST [＿＿] Zip [＿＿＿＿＿] — [＿＿＿＿]

Phone # ([＿＿＿]) [＿＿＿] — [＿＿＿＿] Fax # ([＿＿＿]) [＿＿＿] — [＿＿＿＿]

Email [＿＿＿＿＿＿＿＿＿＿＿＿＿＿＿＿＿＿＿＿＿]

(1) Gender:
＿＿＿ Female ＿＿＿ Male

(2) Age:
＿＿＿ 12 or under ＿＿＿ 40-59
＿＿＿ 13-19 ＿＿＿ 60+
＿＿＿ 20-39

(3) Marital Status
＿＿＿ Married
＿＿＿ Single
＿＿＿ Divorced/Widowed

(4) Did you receive this book as a gift?
＿＿＿ Yes ＿＿＿ No

(6) How did you find out about this book?
Please fill in ONE.
1) ＿＿＿ Recommendation
2) ＿＿＿ Store Display
3) ＿＿＿ Bestseller List
4) ＿＿＿ Online
5) ＿＿＿ Advertisement
6) ＿＿＿ Catalog/Mailing
7) ＿＿＿ Interview/Review (TV, Radio, Print)

(7) Where do you usually buy books?
Please fill in your top TWO choices.
1) ＿＿＿ General Bookstore
2) ＿＿＿ Christian Bookstore
3) ＿＿＿ Online
4) ＿＿＿ Book Club/Mail Order
5) ＿＿＿ Price Club (Costco, Sam's Club, etc.)
6) ＿＿＿ Retail Store (Target, Wal-Mart, etc.)

(9) What subjects do you enjoy reading about most? Rank only **FIVE**. *Use 1 for your favorite, 2 for second favorite, etc.*

	1	2	3	4	5
1) Parenting/Family	○	○	○	○	○
2) Relationships	○	○	○	○	○
3) Recovery/Addictions	○	○	○	○	○
4) Health/Nutrition	○	○	○	○	○
5) Christian Living	○	○	○	○	○
6) Inspiration	○	○	○	○	○
7) Business Self-Help	○	○	○	○	○
8) Teen Issues	○	○	○	○	○
9) Sports	○	○	○	○	○

(14) What attracts you most to a book?
(Please rank 1-4 in order of preference.)

	1	2	3	4
1) Title	○	○	○	○
2) Cover Design	○	○	○	○
3) Author	○	○	○	○
4) Content	○	○	○	○

TAPE IN MIDDLE; DO NOT STAPLE

**NO POSTAGE
NECESSARY
IF MAILED
IN THE
UNITED STATES**

BUSINESS REPLY MAIL
FIRST-CLASS MAIL   PERMIT NO 45   DEERFIELD BEACH, FL

POSTAGE WILL BE PAID BY ADDRESSEE

FAITH COMMUNICATIONS
3201 SW 15TH STREET
DEERFIELD BEACH FL 33442-9875

FOLD HERE

Which Faith Communications book are you currently reading?

Comments:

3. They were *ungodly and immoral.* The Israelites were so immersed in their sin and drunkenness that when Moses and Joshua reentered the camp, the people were literally naked in the open for all their enemies to see.[4]

4. They had *unbelieving spirits.* We know that without faith it is impossible to please God,[5] yet the Israelites chose the security of their fears over the security of God's promise that He would give them the Promised Land. They believed the faithless report of the fleshly scouts and disregarded the faith-filled reports of Joshua and Caleb. As a result, they were excluded from the purposes of God.[6]

5. The Israelites in the wilderness had *ungrateful hearts.* God had provided food, manna in the wilderness and a way out of no way, yet they still complained against God. I want to ask you this question: How much is enough? And how blessed do you expect to be? And at what point do you stop asking for more blessings and begin thanking God for the blessings that He has already given to you?

Seduced by Hidden Enemies Within

The Israelites had been seduced by hidden enemies within, not by a hostile force attacking them from the outside. They lost their lives and their destiny because of these internal enemies— rebellion, idolatry, immorality, unbelief and ungratefulness within their hearts.

The Israelites watched while God made a way out of no way

for them when they were slaves in Egypt. They watched Him break Pharaoh's stubborn will through plague after plague until he was forced to say, "Let the people go." They were there when God raised up Moses, and they saw him stretch his rod over the Red Sea and make it part in a way that allowed the entire nation to cross the Red Sea on dry ground. Then they watched as God released the pent-up waters of the Red Sea to drown Pharaoh and his armies.

Yet even though they "got over" the obstacle of the Red Sea, God was not pleased with many of the Israelites, for they had deceived themselves through their hardness of heart. The same Israelites that God delivered from the yoke of oppression in Egypt misplaced their faith in golden idols once they crossed over. Most of us get deceived once we "get over" some major difficulty or circumstance. When our backs are against the wall, we cry out, "God! Help me, please." But once the crisis passes, so does our intense desire for God's presence and power. Once God makes a way to get us over our impassable obstacle—once we get blessed, qualify for that mortgage, receive the loan, earn the degree, marry our mate, pick up the car or land the promotion— we say by our actions, if not by our words, "So long, God. It's been great *using* You."

The problem with this kind of deception is that it is nearly impossible to know you are being deceived; that is why they call it deception. This has been Satan's favorite tool since he used it to deceive Eve and Adam in the garden of Eden.[7] And he is still such an effective deceiver that Paul made sure we knew the secret of his evil power by saying, "Satan transforms himself as an angel of light."[8] He *looks* right, but he isn't.

Deceit Can Destroy from the Inside Out

Satan is a deceiver and a liar; Jesus called him a liar and the father of lies.[9] When the chief liar dispatches a spirit of deception to a church, his diabolical goal is simple: Get the sheep to destroy one another with "friendly fire." Deceit can destroy a church from the inside out faster and more efficiently than any force attacking from the outside in. The same is true for marriage relationships and lifelong friendships.

Israel had seen God move in unparalleled signs and wonders, but the Israelites became deceived in their callousness and indifference to the things of God. They lost their wonder over the majesty of God. They began to become too *familiar* with the presence of God and with His mighty miracle-working power. They lost their godly fear. Their holy God and His *Shekinah,* or revealed presence, became "common" to them. All this led to a fatal disrespect for the Creator.

This happens in our churches every Sunday. When we first entered the kingdom of God, we were overcome with grateful wonder, awe and joy every time someone got saved. Now all we do when someone gets saved is pop gum and rub our eyes in boredom, just hoping all the excitement down front won't lengthen the service. We have lost the wonder of the glory of God.

This is the problem: When you begin to lose the wonder, it is not long before the Holy Spirit is grieved and God no longer visits your meetings. My friend, when you can look at the wonder of God and not be moved, you should beware—you are on your way to serious trouble. You are becoming calloused and too familiar with the King of Glory. A spirit of negativity toward the deeper things of God will begin to creep in.

Once you forget where you came from and who carried you out of that pit, you become ungrateful and indifferent. It is only a short journey from there to impatience with the Almighty and the worship of false gods such as career, the excessive accumulation of wealth or self-gratification through drugs, illicit sex and the headlong pursuit of pleasure.

Most Church Splitters Think
They Are Doing the Right Thing

Have you checked your spirit lately? When deception enters your heart, you begin to think you could do things better than anyone else. Do you remember Absalom, King David's favorite son? Absalom had a deceiving spirit, and I don't think he even knew it. He probably thought he was doing the right thing (most church splitters do too). Absalom used deception to steal the kingdom from David, his father.

Absalom strategically positioned himself to intercept people on their way to the king's court to present their needs, problems or complaints. He would tell them, "I know you're going over to see my father, King David, and that's fine. *But if I were king,* I have to tell you that I would run things in this way."

The modern versions of this ancient deception all have the same ring to them: "Now, *if I were pastor,* I have to tell you I'd probably treat you differently. I suppose you know that he doesn't recognize your unique gifts and abilities as I do. . . . *If I were the boss,* I would immediately promote you to supervisor of your area. He's the choir director, but *if I had any say in the matter,* you would be the soloist right now. He's the president, *but if I had his authority,* I would make sure you got the loan you really need. *If I were team leader,* I'd make sure your idea was put at the top of the list."

Deceivers love to intercept people *before* they reach the real thing, whether they are on their way to seek God's face, talk to their pastor, attend choir practice or meet with the boss.

Aggressive "Absaloms" (male or female) can steal spouses, friendships, churches and kingdoms with their subtle flattery. They exhibit a cunning ability to identify personal hurts and longings, and they have a devilish willingness to tell people what they want to hear.

Does that sound familiar? It should. We've seen it all described in the events that occurred in the Garden of Eden.

Don't Give Satan a Protected Place

Deception can quickly become transformed from a fleeting thought into a stronghold in our lives—if we allow it to. A stronghold is a spiritual fortress founded upon wrongful thoughts. It gives the enemy of your soul *a protected place of influence* in your life.

The apostle Paul told us how to deal with strongholds. He said, "For the weapons of our warfare are not carnal but mighty in God for pulling down strongholds, casting down arguments and every high thing that exalts itself against the knowledge of God, bringing every thought into captivity to the obedience of Christ."[10]

You will never tear down strongholds with fists, bows and arrows, knives or guns. You attack them with prayer and fasting, with God's Word, through worship and by fulfilling your calling faithfully one day at a time *in unity* with others.

If we do these things in total dependence upon God and give Him the glory in all things, we will pull down every stronghold trying to block our way to victory! It doesn't matter whether we are facing strongholds of bitterness, anger, lust or fear; the anointing of God will break apart every yoke.

Each of us has endured something that has left us with scars, whether we were mistreated or abused as children, were victimized by racial discrimination, beaten by a spouse or betrayed by a close friend. No matter what they are, the arch deceiver will try to use areas of past pain to build himself a stronghold of evil in our lives. Some of us have held on to grievances and wrongs for fifteen or twenty years, and Satan is having a heyday!

"I just . . . I got a right to be angry!"

"No, find that in the Scriptures."
"Honey, I got a right to cuss you out."

Maybe you do feel you have a right to cuss someone out once or twice. It doesn't matter. For your own sake, and because God commands it, give it up and forgive the wrong. Enough is enough. Get over it, and get free.

Don't allow the bad things that happened to you yesterday to become strongholds imprisoning your tomorrows. They can become so familiar that you will wear those strongholds "on your sleeve" like a close friend. They will infiltrate your personality, your family, your church and your future. A spiritual stronghold is a spiritual disease that undermines ministry and relationships. It is like a cancer that sucks the life out of a church or marriage from the inside out. Its two major components are bad attitudes and bad actions.

I am not surprised when people outside the Church and new believers don't understand how "mature" Christians can say "the joy of the Lord is my strength," yet look like they have been baptized in pickle juice all the time. Something doesn't match in this picture.

If you are going to talk the talk, then you had better walk the walk! Anything less is pure hypocrisy, and that particular problem has caused many a church to dry up and die.

A Bad Attitude Spreads Like a Deadly Virus

If you don't expose a bad attitude and kill it quickly, it will soon produce a bad action. Then other people see the action, the devil gets glorified and the whole thing just snowballs. Before you know it, that attitude has spread throughout the Church like a deadly virus or like a cancer that is spreading to other vital organs of its victim's body.

This explains why God's Word tells us, "Be angry, and do not sin: do not let the sun go down on your wrath, nor give place to the devil."[11] You are *never* justified in going to bed angry: all that does is sow seeds of anger and unforgiveness. You might just as well start a small fire in your kitchen before you go to bed and tell yourself, "Oh, I'll put out the flames tomorrow."

We need to kill the disease of deception and uproot our hidden sins wherever we see them. Otherwise we could hinder the hand of God through our sin. God wants to move through His Church; there are crack addicts who need to be delivered. There are prostitutes who need to be saved, marriages that need to be restored and lives in bondage that need to be delivered. Jesus has a whole lot more He wants to do in the local church, so we don't have time to let disease come in.

We don't have time to be jealous of one another. It is time to be delivered through aggressive means. When you are sick and you know there is something going on in your body, you must attack it aggressively. If something is trying to destroy your family, don't sit down and wait for the inevitable. Fight it aggressively. If something is trying to destroy your church, then turn up the prayer power, raise up the praise and power up the anointing of the Holy Spirit!

Make What Is Wrong Right

Let me assure you that if you are part of an effective ministry, then the enemy *will attempt* to come against you in some way. That is your signal to go on the offensive. If you are trying to get it together, and if you are human, then I can guarantee you that the deceiver will be working overtime to see that your happy family in Christ flies apart. Don't be naive—expect to face challenges, and expect the God of creation to be with you every step of the way as you overcome those challenges in Jesus' name. When something goes wrong, don't walk out on the family. Just say, "Well, evidently there's a problem here. Since I am in the family, let me roll up my sleeves and make what's wrong right. After all, we are family."

Do what you know to do and entrust the rest to God. He has no problem separating the fake from the authentic and the right from the wrong. God has a way of turning the light on to what is evil, and He unerringly separates the evil from that which is righteous. Do you recall the benediction in the Book of Jude?

Now unto him that is able *to keep you from falling, and to present you faultless before the presence of his glory with exceeding joy, to the only wise God our Saviour, be glory and majesty, dominion and power, both now and ever. Amen. (Jude 24–25, emphasis mine)*

Remember one fact above all others as you press through life's pressure points and handle the enemies within: *God is able!* He is able to keep you from falling. He is able to keep you from stumbling. He is able to keep you from being deceived and diseased, and from being disconnected from your spiritual family. *He is able to make a way where there is no way.*

Contrary to popular opinion, God is even able to keep the Church together! He is able to restore your joy, preserve your mind and handle any and every enemy that would stand against His will and pleasure for your life. Rest assured, God Almighty will defend His own every time.

I do not want you to make the mistake that Israel made. Never lose the wonder and excitement you have simply in "knowing God." If you sense that the wonder is already gone, there is hope! The way you get the wonder back is to *look back.*

Look back at what you were and at what you didn't have. Now compare them with what you are now because of Jesus, and consider what you *do* have now. Remember life without the rich Christian fellowship, when you should have been dead and gone. Look at what the Lord has done, and the wonder will come again.

Sometimes you will recover your wonder in some of God's simple gifts. I remember one night when I was praying with my children and the wonder of it all just hit me. When I couldn't finish my prayer, my children stopped praying and looked up at me. "What's wrong?" they asked. "Nothing," I said. "Everything is *right,* and that's why I'm crying."

— Endnotes

[1] 1 Cor. 10:5–6, italics mine.

[2] Hosea 4:6a.

[3] Num. 14:10a.

[4] Ex. 32:25.

[5] Heb. 11:6.

[6] Num. 14:28–39.

[7] Gen. 3:1–6.

[8] 2 Cor. 11:14.

[9] John 8:44.

[10] 2 Cor. 10:4–5.

[11] Eph. 4:26–27.

6

Jealousy and Envy

What enemy could threaten the lives and ministries of such legendary leaders as Moses, King David, Daniel, Paul the apostle and even Jesus Christ Himself? Beware, for that same enemy lurks in the shadows of your life and in the lives of those around you even as you read these words! This hidden enemy can explode like flammable gas exposed to a flame, destroying in one violent burst a lifetime of diligent work. Many in the English-speaking world call this enemy the green-eyed monster. It is a venomous beast with two parts—jealousy and envy.

This enemy is so volatile that it has caused many of us to nearly forfeit the inheritance God has ordained for our lives. This happens when we get bound up or compromised by envy and jealousy, when we become so preoccupied with the blessings of someone else's life that we fail to focus on the God who longs to bring us into our own.

Moses was confronted by his own sister and brother, Miriam

and Aaron, after the monster of envy gained control of their hearts. David was haunted by the malignant jealousy eating away at King Saul's heart. Years later, David's own son, Absalom, tried to steal his father's throne for himself. Daniel risked death when jealousy and envy possessed the hearts of his two fellow counselors to the King of Persia. No one is immune to the evils of jealousy and envy.

The mission of Jesus was endangered by jealousy and envy, which threatened to divide His disciples only days before He was to lay down His life on the cross. In the end, it was jealousy and envy that drove the high priests and Jewish Sanhedrin to do the unthinkable and send the Messiah to His death at the hands of Roman soldiers.

Jealousy and envy often thrive when we fail to understand that other people in God's kingdom are different from us because they are at different seasons in their lives. This pattern also shows up in secular settings such as the workplace, the neighborhood gym, the union hall or city hall. Jealousy and envy will thrive in any environment where they find willing hearts.

Some people are deep in their *spring* or *planting season,* a time marked by great hopes, labor-intensive efforts, extreme focus, increased pressures and very little free time or "fruits" to show for all their labor.

The most envied people in God's kingdom are those in their *summer* or *harvest season.* This is when they begin to reap a harvest from the multitude of seeds they sowed long ago.

People in their *autumn season* are beginning to see things drop away from their lives and ministries. Although green still surrounds them, their inner springs of joy seem to be ebbing or pulling back. They sense that they are preparing to enter a time of trial or difficulty, and they are slow to branch out into new things.

People in their *winter season* have less activity in their lives. They may feel that there is very little life or hope in their world. The only thing they have to hold on to is the faithfulness of God and His promise that "this, too, shall pass." (This is the "stretching" season in which we tend to grow the most in terms of faith, maturity and assurance in the faithfulness of God.)

We are all in different seasons, and we have different gifts, qualities and abilities as well. The good news is that God loves us all the same. This also explains why it is so dangerous to covet, to envy or to yield to jealousy over another person's blessings or achievements.

It is too late in the season of God for you and I to get tripped up and cut off from our divine destiny because of jealousy and envy. *Jealousy* causes you to become bitter because of what others have. *Merriam-Webster's Collegiate Dictionary* says jealousy means to be "intolerant of rivalry or unfaithfulness" and to be "hostile toward a rival or one believed to enjoy an advantage."[1] *Envy* causes you to wish you had what someone else has. *Merriam-Webster's* says envy is a "painful or resentful awareness of an advantage enjoyed by another joined with a desire to possess the same advantage."[2]

The Grass on the Other Side
Has to Be Mowed Too!

The tenth commandment tells us not to covet or enviously desire what belongs to our neighbor. God's Word specifically tells us not to covet our neighbor's house, his wife, his servants or his ox and donkey.[3] In modern times, you can add to this list your neighbor's shoes and wardrobe, Mercedes Benz or Jaguar, stock portfolio and corporate or community position.

Much of the destruction and division within the Body of Christ can be traced directly to unchecked jealousy and envy. We need to remember that possessions won't make us happy for long. True contentment is found only in God.

We Americans have a dangerous habit of comparing ourselves to others. We compare spouses, figures, hairstyles, annual incomes, vehicles, children, job status, jewelry, club memberships, educational achievements, retirement funds and even the square footage of our homes. It is ironic: the moment we die, all these things will simply cease to matter. Besides that grim fact, the grass always looks greener on the other side . . . until you get there and realize that *it has to be mowed too.*

When Good People Do Bad Things

Sometimes Christians covet because of the basic human need to be noticed and valued by others. They struggle with their own sense of self-esteem and fall victim to jealousy or envy along the way.

Aaron and Miriam were good people and they were prayerful—they were the equivalent of vice presidents or bishops—but their jealousy and envy toward their brother Moses caused them to do an evil thing.

Miriam was recognized as a prophetess and leader of the Israelites. She was the older sister of Moses who watched him on the river Nile when he was an infant and then observed him rise to prominence and authority as an adopted son of Pharaoh.

Aaron was Moses' older brother and the man God appointed to be His spokesman for Moses before Pharaoh and the first of a long line of high priests.

Despite these credentials, achievements and family connections, jealousy and envy crept into the lives of Miriam and Aaron and nearly destroyed them.

The Bible says Miriam and Aaron "spoke against Moses because of the Ethiopian woman whom he had married."[4] Perhaps the root of the controversy is revealed in what they actually said: "'Has the LORD indeed spoken only through Moses? Has He not spoken through us also?' And the LORD heard it."[5]

Perhaps the real issue was the jealousy and envy Miriam and Aaron felt toward Moses' position and authority as the most powerful leader in Israel. God had used him to lead all Israel across the Red Sea and had delivered to him the Ten Commandments on Mount Sinai. The interracial marriage issue appears to have been a smoke screen used to disguise the real problem.

Miriam especially seemed to have a serious problem with

jealousy and envy. She kept her thoughts to herself *until* Moses showed up with a foreign wife with dark skin. This provided an opportunity for Miriam to express what had been stewing inside her all along. This was an opportunity to criticize for personal advantage. (God always looks at the motive of the heart, no matter how noble the outward claim or cause appears to be.)

The devil is always trying to find an opportunity for evil. When Moses finally returned to Egypt after marrying the Ethiopian woman (the daughter of Jethro, the High Priest of Midian), Miriam was no longer the most important woman in his life. As for Aaron, even though he occupied a high position in Israel and wielded great authority, the real issue was that he was *not* Moses.

Have you ever heard the saying, "Familiarity breeds contempt"? There is a certain amount of truth in it. Miriam and Aaron had become so familiar with Moses that all they could see were what they believed to be his wrong choices. They were blind to the fact that *God was listening* to their complaints. The Lord defends those who are humble and meek before Him, but He resists the proud.[6]

People in this condition often get upset when people they know experience a breakthrough or climb out of their difficulty somehow: "I could celebrate with you over your success and achievement for a moment, but honestly, I was happier when I had to pray for you after you lost your job. I was happier when I had to take money out my pocket to keep food on your table." Isn't it amazing how we can mourn with those who mourn, but we often find it difficult to rejoice with those who rejoice?

Before we criticize someone, we need to pause and think long about our motives. What is motivating you to talk about this person? Are you prepared to reap what you sow? Wisdom tells us to not get caught up in that vicious circle. Do your job, fulfill your responsibilities "as to the Lord" and promotion will come from Him, not from man.[7]

You Have an Unseen Protector

If you have dedicated your life to the Lord and try to live it out each day, you have an unseen Protector who will turn the tables on people who try to set a "trap" for you in the Church, in the workplace or in the community. You don't have to raise your hand, defend yourself or develop a counterplot against your antagonists.

If you have lived long enough, you know what I am talking about. You may have seen God turn the tables on the very individuals who did their best to make you look bad to your boss or leader. Perhaps you were unexpectedly promoted to supervisor over the same people whose false accusations created problems for you when you asked to take off on Sundays and during special church functions. Promotion comes from God for those who trust Him in all things.

So-called constructive criticism is one of the "fruits," or by-products, of jealousy and envy. In reality, these "helpful comments" often amount to little more than words of destructive jealousy masked with a candy coating.

Most of us learn early in childhood that the easiest and quickest way to raise our own status is to bring someone else down with critical words and actions. The Word of God teaches us the opposite. Nevertheless, criticism and negative scheming are seen as the primary tools of advancement by many adults in the business world and workplace. This is what we mean by the expression, "It's a dog-eat-dog world."

Criticism is a technique that does not require talent, intelligence, diligence or valuable work skills. An illiterate six-year-old child can criticize and ridicule the wisest men of the age, but that doesn't mean he or she knows anything about life, wisdom or knowledge.

People pull out the destructive tool of ridicule and criticism when they feel intimidated by someone else who looks more blessed or prosperous than they are. Their actions are rooted in insecurity and a fractured self-concept that can be cured only through a life-changing encounter with Jesus Christ. You and I need to remember this every time we come under fire by self-appointed critics, antagonists and enemies.

Envy destroys the envier and threatens to hamper any relationship he or she may have with God and the Christian community. Envious jealousy is a green-eyed monster, a deadly disease that issues from the pit of hell itself. It spreads voraciously like a malignant tumor attempting to suck the life out of every vital area of its host—whether it is a person, a local church body or an association of churches.

For these reasons, every believer must be quick to act when they see the disease of envy and jealousy begin to surface in the Church. It must be exposed and destroyed at the root before it spreads and multiplies to fatal proportions.

This Spiritual Disease Has a Very Grim Prognosis

Unfortunately, the disease of envy and jealousy is often spawned in the tender places of family relationships and childhood. The disease has a very grim prognosis, and a seed of it is planted every time a parent makes the horrible mistake of comparing one child to another. This triggers a vengeful rivalry that can produce a full-scale outbreak of jealousy and envy that can even destroy the family as the children approach adulthood.

The green-eyed monster also thrives wherever people indulge in petty prejudices and put-downs about ethnic origin, skin color, economic status, body shape or social status. None of these characteristics are given to us by our request; we are simply what we are. Nevertheless, insecure people insist on making themselves feel better by belittling people who are different from them.

Much is made of the prejudice shown toward African Americans by other races in the United States, and this is a valid fact socially and historically. However, many outside the African American community do not know that we hold our own secret prejudices based on skin color that are nothing less than sin. The sad truth is that a special favor tends to be shown toward light-skinned African American children that is withheld from their darker brothers and sisters, with terrible consequences. Even parents are tempted to show more favor toward their children with lighter skin tones than those with darker skin. It is nothing less than foolishness "gone to seed." Nevertheless, I have seen the same prejudice among Africans in South Africa as well as in Amsterdam in the Netherlands. Such foolishness shouldn't exist at all—especially in the house of God!

"The Last One Picked"

Teachers and coaches can reinforce such negative, deep-rooted stereotypes by comparing one student with another and by encouraging unhealthy forms of competition in the extreme. Competition can be healthy and is a normal part of life. However, when competition is fostered and encouraged without limits or corrective measures to ensure healthy self-concepts for all the children involved, the results can be deadly.

Nearly everyone can recall feeling embarrassed and ashamed when they were lined up for the selection of sports teams. You knew you were going to be the last person picked if you were unfortunate enough to have buck teeth, wore thick glasses or were pigeon-toed, slightly uncoordinated or different from most of the other kids. You don't have to imagine what that kind of needless trauma can do in the hearts and minds of children.

The slaughter of self-esteem continues into adulthood. Many of us face brutal performance evaluations on the job that often compare us unfairly to someone else. Women face the peculiar indignities unique to beauty contests, and men are left to find their way in a society that worships the perfect bodies of male models and athletes—even though the Creator didn't seem to be so concerned with such fat-free curves when He made most of the men on this planet. The list of stereotypes and unrealistic expectations goes on and on, as does the litany of destruction in its wake.

Enough is enough. It is time to do things God's way. We need to understand what God thinks about jealousy and envy, because this knowledge will help us avoid a great deal of needless grief in our lives.

When Miriam and Aaron allowed their jealousy and envy of Moses to come to full fruit in their challenge to Moses' God-given authority and position, two things happened: First, God heard them. Second, He called both accusers and the accused to stand before Him.

It is interesting to note that Moses didn't say a single word during this encounter until *after* God had dealt with Miriam. And when he finally began to speak, he didn't defend himself or direct well-deserved counteraccusations at his accusers; instead he asked God to forgive and heal Miriam.[8]

Jealousy and envy do not belong in the family of God, because they always cause us to pull each other down; what God commands us to do is to support one another. His directive is to continually build up those around us while strengthening our bonds of love and mutual concern.

It is easier to mourn with those who mourn than to rejoice

with those who rejoice when deep down we resent their blessings, prosperity and elevated position. When envy and jealousy are not exposed and promptly destroyed, they begin to subtly plant resentment in our hearts toward others.

Gradually, our demeanor changes from sweet to sour, and our "spiritual complexion" begins to take on the telltale green tint of this disease. A bitter aftertaste of divisive envy begins to invade our sweet fellowship. The smiles and hearty "amens" may still be there, but beneath the surface a deadly root has taken hold of a heart at risk.

As a member of God's household who attends a local church, you have a solemn responsibility to look out for the safety of your spiritual family and each of its members in particular. When you start hearing negative, critical comments and sly innuendoes, accompanied by the equally critical glances and contemptuous stares that signal the presence of a green-eyed monster, what will you do?

In that very moment, you need to kill it at the root. Now I am *not* talking about killing people; I am referring to the spread of evil words and destructive attitudes. Don't try to "kill it sweetly" with some politically correct statement such as, "Well, everybody has an opinion."

Stating a personal opinion is one thing, but it is another thing to willfully sow or spread what the Bible calls "seeds of discord." Once you decide to voice your opinion in a way or setting that tears down leaders and fellow believers or separates the Body of Christ, you can count on God hearing your words. Those who sow discord are specifically listed on God's "hate and hit list" because of the extreme danger they pose to His precious sheep, the Church. It is a fearful thing to fall into the hands of an angry God.

Take clear and decisive action when you detect the presence of jealousy and envy. For example, if you are seated in the barbershop, beauty salon or restaurant and a staff member speaks in a way that is offensive to you and disrespectful to our faith, you need to interrupt that person and say:

> *Sir/Ma'am, excuse me. You are entitled to your opinion, but you are not entitled to offend what is sacred to me like that. I'm sorry, but you will have to take away this food. Cancel my order. It is clear that I will have to take my business around the corner to the next establishment. I refuse to spend my money and time in a place where someone runs down my church and my Lord—the Church is sacred and holy to me. It is my praying ground, the pillar and ground of the truth.*

Some of us don't have a blessed thing because we've spent our lives criticizing the local church and God's anointed leaders. Don't expect God to bless your mess if you insist on speaking against the things and people of His kingdom. God's Church is holy, and so are the people who comprise it.

When Miriam spoke against God's anointed leader, He dealt with her swiftly and severely, even though she was a prophetess and a proven leader herself. I can hear the skeptic saying, "Well, maybe Moses deserved it. Was he perfect or something?"

The Bible doesn't say Moses was perfect. If you read the Book of Exodus—or any other book for that matter—you will notice that the Bible is brutally honest. God makes it clear that Moses was human and flawed like everybody else. However, he was God's anointed, His chosen leader, and he was humble and faithful before God. Once God struck Miriam with leprosy, only the prayer of Moses was able to get her healed.

Praying for My Accusers

I can identify with how Moses must have felt. As a pastor, I have been called to critical care units in hospitals to lay hands on individuals who I knew had criticized me and had caused problems in the local church. My flesh wasn't very happy about it, but God still required me to pray for my accusers in faith and humility.

One of the little-known side effects of the disease of jealousy and envy is its tendency to destroy our confidence in our own abilities and worth. Insecure people who are consumed with envy and jealousy are compulsive about comparing themselves with other people. No matter which way you look at it, the decision to criticize is always a lose-lose situation.

Envy has an ancient track record for destroying relationships. It is fine for people to compete in sports contests, games and in the naturally competitive realm of commerce and trade as long as biblical standards of conduct and ethics are observed. However, there are certain places and situations where competition has no place. The Church is one of them.

God's Word clearly establishes the *right way* to deal with other believers in the Church:

> *Fulfill ye my joy, that ye be likeminded, having the same love, being of one accord, of one mind.* Let nothing be done through strife or vainglory; *but in lowliness of mind let each esteem others better than themselves. Look not every man on his own things, but every man also on the things of others. (Phil. 2:2–4 KJV, emphasis mine)*

In spite of that clear command, many Bible-believing churches in North America and around the world are literally competing against one another for members. Other churches advertise themselves as a prominent national ministry, with or without national relevancy. They are simply local churches. God is not pleased when this happens, no matter who is involved. How many ways does He have to say that we are all in this thing together?

Travel Tips for the Rough Road of Reality

James was the disciple who excelled in the practical aspects of the Christian life. He had a way of cutting through all the theology to where the "rubber tires of daily practice meet the rough road of reality." The apostle James said:

> *Who is a wise man and endued with knowledge among you? Let him show out of a good conversation his works with meekness of wisdom. But if ye have bitter envying and strife in your hearts, glory*

not, and lie not against the truth. This wisdom descendeth not from above, but is earthly, sensual, devilish. For where envying and strife is, there is confusion and every evil work. (3:13–16 KJV)

If you frequently find fault with others and if you find it difficult or impossible to rejoice with those who rejoice, examine your heart carefully. If you discover that you have envy and jealousy in your heart, then admit it, expose it and kill it quickly. The good news is that God always has a way of escape. Deliverance begins when you are honest about the green-eyed monster of envy and jealousy, because envy has many disguises.

The final step is repentance. Go to the Lord in prayer and openly confess your sins of envy and jealousy. Then pray:

Lord, forgive me for my sins and help me fight this green-eyed monster of jealousy and envy. It seems like every time I kill it, it tries to come back. Because of my human condition, I need Your divine help to defeat envy and jealousy on a daily basis.

Lord, help me to clearly see and appreciate what You have done and the things You have given to me. I want to thank You because I'm alive and because my lifeblood is running warm in my veins. Thank You for waking me up this morning and clothing me in my right mind. In Jesus' name I honor and thank You. Amen.

— Endnotes

1 *Merriam-Webster's Collegiate Dictionary,* 11th ed. (Springfield, MA: Merriam-Webster, Inc., 2003), 671.

2 *Merriam-Webster's Collegiate Dictionary,* 11th ed., 418.

3 Ex. 20:17.

4 Num. 12:1.

5 Num. 12:2.

6 Jas. 4:6.

7 Phil. 2:14–15; Col. 3:23; Ps. 75:6–7.

8 Num. 12:2–13.

7

The Spirit of Murder

I have a mission and a divine assignment to do more than pen a few flowery phrases for a book to delight the soul. My task is not to discuss the financial principles of God's kingdom, although I do believe in them and practice them. The Lord has commanded me to speak of murder and transgenerational intrigue in secret places. He has commissioned me to issue a challenge to you and to the Church.

An evil force is running loose on earth. It has bridged the ages by operating through the lives of willing men and women since the dawn of time. This demonic force entered the thoughts of Egypt's Pharaoh shortly after the birth of Moses. It used irrational fear to force one of the earth's most powerful rulers in that age to order the execution of every Hebrew male child below a certain age! Why? Because Pharaoh was desperate to limit the potential power of Egypt's exploding Hebrew slave population.

The Book of Exodus describes the way God orchestrated a

plan to preserve His people's deliverer and to have Pharaoh himself provide a home and a royal education for the young man
who would one day lead all of the Israelite slaves out of Egypt
and into its divine destiny.

This spirit of murder once again surfaced in a line of wicked
kings descended from Edom in the Middle East. Known to history by the family title of Herod, their number included Herod
Antipas, Herod Antipater and Herod the Great. They all yielded
to this murderous spirit, but none more willingly and with more
tragic results than Herod the Great.

Herod the Great has been dead for more than two thousand
years, yet his name—and the spirit that burned his memory into
history—seems to live on. It was Herod the Great who, in a fit
of paranoia and fear of the rival Jewish king mentioned by visiting wise men from the East, ordered the ruthless slaughter of
every child in Bethlehem who was two years old or younger. This
murderous, demonic spirit that I call the spirit of Herod *still*
seeks to destroy the seed of deliverers.

> *And when [the wise men] were departed, behold, the angel of the*
> *Lord appeareth to Joseph in a dream, saying, Arise, and take the*
> *young child and his mother, and flee into Egypt, and be thou there*
> *until I bring thee word:* for Herod will seek the young child to
> destroy him. . . . *Then Herod, when he saw that he was mocked of*
> *the wise men, was exceeding wroth, and sent forth, and* slew all the
> children that were in Bethlehem, *and in all the coasts thereof, from*
> *two years old and under. . . . (Matt. 2:13, 16 KJV, emphasis mine)*

Mourning Mothers

Wherever this murderous spirit exists, you will find mothers mourning the loss of their children. Mothers mourned in Christ's birthplace after Herod failed to find the infant Jesus and sent out his death squads to kill the innocents of Bethlehem.

Mothers are still mourning for their children today in Washington, D.C., and Harlem, New York. They are mourning in Chicago, Illinois, and they are mourning in the Watts district of Los Angeles. They are mourning in Littleton, Colorado, in Paducah, Kentucky and Jonesboro, Arkansas. They are mourning over the mass killings of innocent people by terrorists at the World Trade Center towers, the Pentagon and in the Pennsylvania jetliner crash. They are mourning over the series of senseless sniper killings in New Jersey, Virginia and Maryland.

Hundreds of mothers are mourning in America today because a spirit of murder and terror is running loose in our streets, in our schools and in our media. It seeks to take away our boys and girls in an evil wave of violence and murder.

Make no mistake: we are dealing with a *spirit of evil*, not simply a few isolated killers who are mentally unstable. This spirit is nourished and nurtured by a plethora of violent video games and the twisted spewings of dark-spirited songwriters who write of death and mayhem and profit from the millions they rake in from American youth. This foul spirit also feeds on the ideas planted in our children's hearts and minds by violent movies, plays and concerts where it is common to see a string of ambulances streaming from the main gate after each performance.

To make matters worse, lax enforcement of laws and massive loopholes in the legal system allow people of any age and background easy access to firearms. Make no mistake, we are faced once again with the spirit of Herod—the spirit of murder and destruction—roaming our streets. What is the answer?

The answer is simple but dramatically effective. The answer is *the blood.* The blood Jesus Christ shed on the cross stands against every principality, power and force of darkness in this moment. God has called the Church to stand and face the spirit of Herod toe-to-toe, not run from it. It is time to declare the promise of Jesus: "The gates of hell shall not prevail against the church."[1]

As Paul said, we are not fighting against flesh and blood.[2] We are dealing with a spirit, an evil entity that can't be seen but can be *felt* by the spiritually aware. You can tell the difference between normal adolescent rebellion and a budding demonic force that is attempting to dominate your child. You also can tell the difference between a normal marital difficulty and a spirit of evil that is determined to destroy yet another home.

In many areas of the United States, it seems as if the spirit of Herod is still ruling and reigning from his throne. It is true that the spirit of Herod has no real authority or power over the Church—if, and I stress *if,* the Church understands its responsibility and the power of the blood of Jesus. Yet this spirit of destruction continues to take its deadly toll in our nation.

All too often we do nothing because we are not aware of Satan's devices (although Paul said we should be!), so we continue to "do the Church house rut" with no regard for the chaos around us.[3] We worship and give God praise every Sunday morning, but during the rest of the week our communities continue to die as mourning mothers attend funeral after funeral and burial after burial.

Young Men Confined to Wheelchairs

Have you noticed how many young men in America's inner cities are confined to wheelchairs? We are seeing an epidemic of these cases. My friend, most of these young men did not land in wheelchairs because of heart disease, complications from the AIDS virus, severe asthmatic problems, diving accidents or muscular dystrophy. This wheelchair epidemic is due to an unprecedented flood of spinal cord injuries suffered from point-blank gunshot wounds.

If you comb the inner-city neighborhoods of Newark, Harlem, Washington, D.C., Houston, Los Angeles and Chicago, you will see countless numbers of our sons, nephews and grandsons bound to wheelchairs as a result of the hellish deeds of people inspired by the spirit of Herod.

This is my challenge and the most important part of my assignment: God has called the Church to confront the spirit of murder unleashed on our nation.

God has equipped us for the battle with *supernatural power*. That is why the disciples were told, "But ye shall receive *power*, after the Holy Ghost is come upon you."[4] He didn't give us such power just so we could have an emotional rush or experience a supernatural manifestation in our bodies. These things are wonderful blessings from God, and the surge of energy is a joyous thing, but the power of the Holy Spirit was never meant to be reserved for our own private "church parties" on Sunday morning. We were "plugged in" to God's power source for a much greater purpose. We are commanded to be bold witnesses for Christ in a world that does not love God and as a result is dying.

We Have the Power to "Confront" It!

The Church was raised up and empowered to *handle* the spirit of the enemy. That means our focus must go beyond any "us four and no more" mentality. This battle is about our children and the generation that will inherit the earth. It is time for us to face the murderous spirit of Herod head-on.

The spirit of Herod can be seen in the New-Age mentality that claims to not need God. This mentality embraces the idea that there can be more than one God or more than one religion. Yet if we choose to abort our faith in God, we position ourselves to fall victim to life's pressure situations. Our children then become unprotected and uncovered. Yes, some of them even die.

This spirit of murder will try to introduce them to drug addiction, alcoholism, pornography or illicit sexual experimentation; or he will destroy their youthful hopes when they stumble, when they encounter failure or the lonely emptiness so common during puberty. He also wants to murder our heavenly dreams and divine visions. He wants to strangle our praise, stifle our witness and bury our future under a mountain of regrets, fears and excuses.

We are called to confront Herod, not run from him. The murderous spirit of Herod didn't stop just because he failed to murder the Son of God when He was still an infant boy. That same spirit of destruction still roams the earth searching for ways to steal, kill and destroy everything that is holy and good. It will use every conceivable human weakness and vice it can find to destroy our children, the next generation of redeemers and deliverers.

God has not only given us *power* to handle Herod, but He is also moving us into the *position* for victory. When the spirit of Herod plotted to kill the infant Jesus, God spoke to Joseph in a dream. This man was *in position* to hear from God, so when he received an early warning about Herod's plot, he listened and he acted. He quickly moved Mary and Jesus to safety in Egypt and remained there until Herod the Great died.

I wish more mothers, fathers and pastors were in position to hear what the Spirit of the Lord is saying today.

Can These Bones Live?

God has given us *power* to handle Herod! We can handle this satanic spirit. God's Word declares that "no weapon formed against us shall prosper."[5] When you are in position, God can speak to you in the middle of the night and reveal the enemy's secret plans. God did this for the prophet Elisha, so why shouldn't He do it for you?[6] Joseph was in position to hear what the Spirit was saying, and he saved the life of the Savior of the world. We need to learn how to hear what the Spirit is saying so we can save a generation of young disciples called to do the works of Jesus.

If you stay in position, you might discover that the Spirit of God will also speak to you about your marriage, your personal integrity or your financial decisions. It always pays to stay in position and listen to what the Spirit of God is saying.

As parents, believers, leaders and citizens of our nation, we stand in the place of Ezekiel the prophet today. We have received power and authority, along with a command. Now God, and His angelic army, is simply waiting on us to *speak the word*. If we are going to confront Satan's spirit of Herod, then we must wake up and understand the importance of our biblical *position* and the power of prophetic declaration.

Too many of us want to take the compromising position that Ezekiel the prophet took just before God pinned him down with a searing question. First the Lord brought Ezekiel to a valley filled with dry bones and had him look at the bones from every angle. Then He asked the prophet a question:

> *"Son of man, can these bones live?"*
> *"O Lord GOD, You know."*
> *Then God said, "No, no, brother. Don't put that back on Me. I asked you the question."*[7]

Resurrecting "What Could Have Been"

As we stare across the spiritually dead expanse of our cities, we see the dry bones of millions of deceased dreams and unfulfilled destinies. We see an entire army of "could have beens" just waiting for the breath of life to revive and reassemble them.

As the Lord God asked Ezekiel so long ago, so today He's asking us, "Sons and daughters of man, can these bones live?" What a powerful question. But so far, all God is hearing from us is the limp reply, "Well, God, I guess *You* know. . . ." Consider the facts: He has already given us the *power* to breathe life into our cities. Now He is waiting for us to step into the prophetic position of victory and speak the words of life to revive our broken dreams, to breathe life once again into the promise we show when we are born. It is time to get busy. God has done His part. Now it is up to us to obey Him and to use His power and provision to save our families, cities and nation from Herod and his destructive power.

I have something important, a divine mandate, to tell you: *There is more in you than you know.* The power of either life or death is in your tongue, so speak life. You may not be an ordained minister, but you were ordained by the power of God on the day Jesus Christ saved you from a life of sin and shame to speak it. You have been given supernatural *power* in Jesus' name. You have been moved into the prophetic position of victory by the Holy Spirit. Now it is time to address the third area of responsibility: It is time to move into position to *protect* those whom God entrusts to us.

Parents, preachers, prophets, educators and church leaders at all levels are called to rescue the perishing, care for the dying and reach out to those who have been left uncovered, unloved and unprotected. However, the first line of protection begins in the home. Once we have moved into a position to hear and obey the leadings of God, we need to take stock of our home base. What is the state of your marriage, of your home and of each of your children? If you don't know, you can be sure you already have a problem. What is the state of your finances? Have you made provision for the future as well as the present? Do you have a godly plan for your family and parenting choices?

What About the Children?

Many of us need to bring our families into "protective custody." If we are called to save the seed, we must reprioritize and realign our lives to preserve what is most precious. Far too many families in the Body of Christ are out of order. Ask yourself, "Who is watching the children while we are having a good time in church?"

Is your teenage son at home, lounging on your living room couch in front of the television? Is your daughter at home losing her virginity while you are out serving the Lord? Don't allow your grandson to hide in a bedroom at home and roll marijuana joints while you're at the altar praying and singing the songs of Zion. God wants us to be vigilant both in prayer *and* in the natural realm. Ask yourself, "What about the children?"

There is a small chance that you are old enough (and fortunate enough) to remember what it was like to grow up in an extended community where your neighbors cared about you almost as much as your parents did. You knew you could get a cup of hot cocoa from a neighbor without any danger of being molested. By the same token, you also could be disciplined by the neighbor and not be worried about being abused. Today, most of our communities are so fragmented and the family unit is so dysfunctional that our children are killing each other in their inner pain and outward rage. They so long for a place to call home that sometimes they create it themselves in the form of a violent, ultraloyal gang. We need to make sure they are not driven to this extreme.

The Church Village:
All-Too-Human Sinners Saved by Grace

We need to reform our understanding of the Church. The Church is actually a refuge—a village of holiness set apart from the greater press of humanity. If you love the Church, then you need to help protect the Church by being faithful in attendance, service, support and prayer. The Church is a village of all-too-human sinners saved by grace. It isn't a place of perfection, but a place where God's mercy and grace may be found.

People in your city or region ought to know that your local church is a place of structure, solace and stability. This can only happen when every concerned member of the local church body makes protection a priority. When good people leave it to someone else, they may discover one day that a pedophile has taken the lead in the church nursery.

Don't misunderstand what I am saying. I believe there is room under the blood of Christ even for *former* pedophiles. The blood of the Lamb covers it all, but none of us has the right to come into Christ's Body and continue our lives of sin and degradation.

True salvation and redemption come only *after* we repent and turn away from our sins. There should always be room in the Church for any sinner who wants to get right, even if it means a long struggle. In the name of Jesus, we will help you through the battle. However, no one should be allowed to corrupt someone else on the way to deliverance!

The Church can truly be a place of protection when God is on the throne (which is eternally true) and God's people are in a position of protection (which is rarely true). If you love God's Church, then get used to keeping your spiritual and natural eyes open.

Check the bathrooms, look into the nursery, take a stroll to the back rooms and the dark corners behind the auditorium and underneath the main floor. Stick your head inside the chapel to make sure everything and everybody is right where they are supposed to be.

The Enemy Would Love
to Send Scandal Your Way

Why am I going on and on with this topic? You may not realize it, but the enemy would love to send some type of scandal your way to ruin the testimony of the entire church body. It takes vigilance and the power of God to handle the spirit of Herod.

God is just looking for believers who want to press in and press through life's pressure points, who will say, "Lord, I want to be willing." The Master stands at the door of *our* hearts: "Behold, I stand at the door, and knock: if any one hears my voice, and opens the door, I will come in to him, and will sup with them, and they with me."[8]

If you are willing, if you want to be in position and you want to bring your children into protective custody, then answer the Master's call. You will have unlimited access to the power of God to fulfill the purpose of your life. If you open the door to God's presence, you will receive the promise of Isaiah the prophet: "Arise, shine; for thy light is come, and the glory of the Lord is risen upon thee."[9]

God is calling for the Church to rise up from her fear and doubt. He wants us to understand that He has given us *power* to handle Herod. He also wants us to understand just how close He is to us in our day-by-day journey of faith. Jesus' last words to His disciples are also His last words to us: "And . . . he breathed on them, and saith unto them, receive ye the Holy Ghost."[10] As He was leaving the earth, He said, "Lo, *I am with you always, even unto the end of the world.*"[11]

He was saying, "I am with you in your parenting. I'm with you in your preaching and prophesying. I'm with you in your warfare and in your work. I'm with you in your struggle and in every single area of your life. You are not alone in life's journey and in your battle with Herod.

Are You Positioned for Victory?

We may not know everything that will come tomorrow, but we do know who holds us in His hand. Have you been dressed with His *power* from on high to proclaim freedom to the captives? You should know that He is patiently moving you into position for victory and He has given you a mandate to preserve and protect those who are at risk.

Every time the world's pundits predict a runaway epidemic of violence and bloodshed in America's streets, we should hold our ground without fear or hesitation. God has given [us] *power to handle Herod* and to confront the powers of evil! We have His eternal promise that "no weapon formed against us shall prosper" and that "greater is He that is in us than he that is in the world."[12]

Finally, we have a responsibility to teach and train our children in godly things, and we must do it as a team, as a heavenly village bound together in love and mutual care one for another. Let us get into position and come together in unified prayer.

As we fight this thing, let us walk and talk together. Let us worship the King together and share our common vision in Christ. It is time to meet the murderous spirit of Herod in power and authority as the glorious Bride of Christ. We should pray our way through life's pressure. Set aside quiet time to hear from

God and He will communicate to you His desire for your life.

"What shall we then say to these things? If God be for us, who can be against us?"[13] It is time to stand together against the spirit of darkness and declare in prophetic prayer:

Father God, we ask in Jesus' name that You forgive us for our prayerlessness. Forgive us for failing to put the right things in our children. Today we have heard the call, and in the name of Jesus we access Your power and step into position to go to war.

By Your grace and power, we step into position and bring our natural and spiritual seed into protective custody. We are not afraid to handle Herod. We refuse to permit that spirit of murder and destruction to launch bullets at our children on neighborhood streets. We won't stand by while little innocent ones are murdered in their beds or on the school playgrounds of our cities.

Enough is enough—the giant of God has awakened from her slumber! Herod, your season of defeat is here. In the name of the risen Lord Jesus Christ, we cast down every vain imagination and defiant spirit. We break the power of darkness over our children and our streets!

With one mind, one accord and one risen Lord, we take authority over every lawless spirit dispatched against the redeemed of God. We loose the angelic hosts of heaven to bring comfort, deliverance, protection and the rule of God to our cities, schools and homes.

We stand now as a holy hedge of protection against the power of the spirit of Herod. We declare, "Satan, the blood of Jesus is against you, and His blood covers our seed."

We also stretch out our hands over the children of this city, of this state and of this nation, and we plead the blood of Jesus over them as well. We declare by the authority given to the Church by the living God that these children shall be protected from the power of Herod. Satan, the blood of Jesus is against you. You have no authority here. The killing will stop. The violence will stop. We so decree peace in every school.

In Jesus' holy name we declare and receive these petitions with thanksgiving and praise. Amen.

— Endnotes ——————————————————

1   Matt. 16:18 KJV.

2   Eph. 6:12.

3   2 Cor. 2:11.

4   Acts 1:8a KJV, italics mine.

5   Isa. 54:17.

6   2 Kings 6:12.

7   This is my version of Ezek. 37:3.

8   Rev. 3:20.

9   Isa. 60:1 KJV.

10 John 20:22 KJV.

11 Matt. 28:20b KJV, emphasis mine.

12 Isa. 54:17; 1 John 4:4 KJV.

13 Rom. 8:31 KJV.

8

The Pressure to Compromise

"No, I will not bow down; even if you threaten to kill me."

What would you do in a moment of supreme temptation and testing? History and experience indicate that most people under pressure quickly shed the truth and compromise their convictions, especially if their lives are on the line.

Most of us hope we would do better than most. We pray that somehow we would have enough inner strength and personal conviction to stand firm and strong in the day of trouble. If it comes to that point, we can take hope from the Bible.

The lives of Elijah, Daniel, David, Moses, Paul, Peter and Stephen indicate that God reveals Himself in a special way to people who face severe persecution or death for His sake. Most of these miracle deliverances, however, seemed to happen only *after* these leaders made the most difficult of all human decisions (without the benefit of knowing how things would eventually turn out).

Daniel the prophet and his three young Hebrew companions had to take a difficult stand after King Nebuchadnezzar of Babylon forcibly relocated them from the royal palace of Judah to his royal court in what is now called Iraq.

The favor of God quickly elevated these young Hebrew men to positions of prominence above virtually everyone else in Babylon—including the king's former chief advisors, who were Babylonians and Chaldeans. This group of discontents became the Hebrews' most dangerous enemies.

When King Nebuchadnezzar made an image of gold and required everyone to bow to it, the three young men from Judah faced a serious problem (the Bible doesn't mention Daniel at this point). They could live if they bowed to the king's false god; but if they remained true to Jehovah and refused to bow their knees, they faced certain death.

Daniel's companions chose to stand for God while everyone else bowed to Nebuchadnezzar's image. Naturally, their enemies made sure the king of Babylon heard about it: "There are *certain Jews* . . . ," they said "[who] have not paid due regard to you. They do not serve your gods or worship the gold image which you have set up."[1]

Who Is the God Who Will Deliver You?

At this news, King Nebuchadnezzar flew into a rage and ordered that Shadrach, Meshach and Abednego be brought before him. The king offered the men a second chance to bow before his golden image and warned them, "But if you do not worship you shall be cast immediately into the midst of a burning fiery furnace. And who is the God who will deliver you from my hands?"[2]

Shadrach, Meshach and Abednego answered the threats of the Babylonian king with these classic words of uncompromising faith:

> *"O Nebuchadnezzar, we have no need to answer you in this matter. If that is the case, our God whom we serve is able to deliver us from the burning fiery furnace, and He will deliver us from your hand, O king. But if not, let it be known to you, O king, that we do not serve your gods, nor will we worship the gold image which you have set up." (Dan. 3:17b–18)*

This is God's blueprint for conduct, and it is a divine survival course for any Christian who is determined to live holy in an unholy age. There is a time and a place for standing on God's promises of deliverance and provision, but the highest and holiest place is the place of total dependence and surrender to the hands and will of God. These young Hebrew men weren't making demands of God or placing conditions on their commitments: they were taking a stand with God, whether He delivered them from the flames or not!

Step into the Position of Submission

God is still sovereign today. It isn't our place to command God to run through hoops or to remove or deliver us from every difficulty. Our place is the position of submission.

It is God who commands *us* to run through hoops and follow Him into the unholy halls of hell to redeem the lost. Where *He* leads, I will follow, the Bible says—not the other way around. We must work within God's designs and speak what God declares.

Our purpose and destiny is found in the center of God's eternal plans and purposes. It does not matter what price we must pay or what persecution comes our way; we must decide to make our stand *before* we face faith's hard demands. Then, when a day of trouble comes, our course is clear, our choice already made.

We can't have it both ways: Either we are Christians or we are not. If we have been transformed by the power of God through Jesus Christ, then our confession is sealed in heaven: "We will not bow down to the enemy's idolatrous images." We said it once, now we'll say it again: "We will not bow."

Perhaps Job said it best when he told his critical friends, "Though He slay me, yet will I trust Him."[3] The epitome of the suffering servant, Job understood that the path he had chosen was not an easy one, and he was determined to stay the course no matter where it led.

Everyone—Christian and non-Christian alike—encounters pressure points in life. Far too many Christians do not know how to press through them.

Persevering Through Hardship

It is one thing to talk about having integrity and courage; it is another thing to deal with the grim reality of compromise. It is deceptively easy to compromise when your back is up against the wall. Godly friends and counselors can make all the difference in those trying times.

God placed us in the divine family called the Church because we all need good friends we can count on in times of trouble. I am talking about people who share your values and morals, and who know your God. Shadrach, Meshach, Abednego and Belteshazzar (Daniel) provide a model of such friendship: they were good friends who persevered through hardship *together*.

Daniel is the central figure and the author of the Book of Daniel. His name means "God is my judge" or "judge of God." When King Nebuchadnezzar captured Judah and the city of Jerusalem, he handpicked sixteen-year-old Daniel and the other three Hebrew youths for governmental service and took them back to Babylon.

For at least sixty years, Daniel served as a leading official in the Babylonian government (and possibly for as long as eighty-four years). It is significant that God used Daniel, anointed him and consecrated him to be His mouthpiece in the midst of a foreign government—even in the position of an unwilling servant to the kings who held his people captive.

God still calls, anoints and appoints people for leadership today. He still promotes and divinely positions His people in high places of influence throughout the societies of the world in this new millennium. And He still has the same unyielding standard for such men and women: they must not compromise what is eternally right for temporal might.

The Higher You Go, the Farther You Can Fall

The degree of your promotion may determine how much pressure you feel to compromise when your back is up against the wall. The Book of Daniel is also an instructional book with timeless truths that are relevant to God's people in every culture, circumstance and era.

As we approach what many believe is the great harvest, some of us may have to endure the same kind of persecution that Shadrach, Meshach and Abednego endured. Perhaps this explains why God is pouring out such glory, power and anointing in our generation. He is preparing and equipping a remnant in the Church that will stand up and boldly declare, "We don't care what we have to do or go through in Christ's name—we will not bow, we will not yield and we will not compromise!"

The Book of Daniel offers us an unparalleled lesson on the power and perils of personal influence and integrity. It also reveals some of the ways God insulates and protects His servants.

Whether we look at Daniel's devotion to prayer in the face of death in the lions' den, or the stand made by his three friends in the face of the king's fiery furnace, these young Hebrew leaders refused to compromise in exchange for the comforts of influence and worldly power. They would not sacrifice their integrity, even when it earned them one-way trips to Nebuchadnezzar's furnace and the lions' den.

The Lord Jesus joined the three Hebrew youths in the midst of the furnace and insulated them from the fire so they could hold a praise meeting right in front of the king. He sent an angel to shut the mouths of the king's lions on Daniel's behalf. That means, my friend, that Jesus will show up for you too—in your fiery trials and the hot situations you find yourself in.

Sometimes God places His leaders in key situations where they can influence the direction of entire nations. God used Daniel as a prophetic voice and a visionary, to speak into the life of King Nebuchadnezzar.

A Direct Line to the Divine Mind

The king of Babylon would have felt right at home in modern America, with its twenty-four-hour psychic hotlines and "dial-a-fortune" soothsayers. This pagan king routinely consulted with sorcerers, yet even he discovered that God's prophet had a direct line to the divine mind.

The difference between Daniel and the psychics of his day was that his revelation came directly from God, not from familiar spirits. Daniel couldn't be bought and he spoke only when God spoke to him. Familiar spirits are like bad relationships that linger in our lives. Racism and sexism also contribute to our society's ills, to a conscience that prohibits us from functioning in a clean and progressive fashion.

Nebuchadnezzar quickly realized that Daniel had an inside track and a word of sure prophecy. We are told that he promoted Daniel because there was "an excellent spirit" in him.[4] God's favor shines on us even in the midst of apparent captivity and adversity: when you have His favor, nothing else matters.

When you step into a situation at His command by faith, you will find doors opening for no known reason. Grants, loans, mortgages and favor with high officials come through divine favor—even if the individuals involved can't explain why they are doing what they are doing. When this happens, the favor of God is at work. Daniel and his three young protégés had God's favor; so, despite the best efforts of their enemies to destroy them, they survived.

King Nebuchadnezzar and his officials followed the pattern of conquerors in that day by giving their captives names that mocked their beliefs and belittled them. Hananiah, whose name meant "Jah has favored," was renamed Shadrach meaning "circuit of the sun."[5] Mishael, Hebrew for "Who is what God is?" received the name Meshach or "Who is what Aku is?"[6] (Aku was a Babylonian deity.) Azariah, a Hebrew name meaning "Jah has helped," was renamed Abednego, or "servant of Nego."[7] (Nego was the Babylonian god of fire.) And Daniel, whose name meant "judge of God" or "God is my judge," was renamed Belteshazzar, which means "he whom Bel favors."[8] (Bel was "Baal," or chief fertility god of the Babylonians.)

You Can Change Our Names but Not Our Hearts!

Nebuchadnezzar and other conquerors in the Middle East of antiquity felt there was genuine power in a name. For that reason, they changed the names of their prisoners and slaves in order to change, break or reroute their influence and loyalty. Daniel and his three young Hebrew friends managed to say, through the example of their lives, "You can change our names, but you will never change our hearts!"

We need to walk in this revelation as we move deeper into this new millennium and declare to every adversary who confronts us, "You may change my name; you may alter my diet, move me from one neighborhood to another or rob me of my natural heritage; but *you cannot change my heart.* You need to hold faith to this truth: 'My hope is fixed on nothing less than Jesus' blood and righteousness.'"

What God has anointed, no man can "un-anoint." Whom God has consecrated or set apart, no man or system can set aside. If the Lord has called me, then I am called. If the Lord has given me favor, I have favor. If the Lord protects me, then I am protected. If the Lord is blessing me, then I am blessed. You cannot curse what God has blessed!

The Word of God declares, "For God has not given us a spirit of fear, but of power and of love and of a sound mind."[9]

Hold the Best and Learn from the Rest

God intends for the Church to hold to the best things received from previous generations, while learning from the rest. If we want to press through for Christ in this new millennium, then we must reaccess some of the old ways of previous generations. In particular, we need to reclaim the seriousness and discipline that our elders possessed forty years ago, without the external, "clothesline religion" that forbade pants, lipstick, earrings or nice hairstyles for women while imposing virtually no restrictions on men.

We must embrace a new level of commitment to the Christ of the Gospel as we move closer to the second coming of the Lord Jesus. He is coming back looking for a church without spot or wrinkle; and frankly, we have a few wrinkles to be ironed out. The spirit of seduction and compromise has flooded our society and isolated those saints who refuse to compromise.

We face the same call to uncompromised righteousness that Shadrach, Meshach and Abednego heard thousands of years ago. They were people of influence faced with great pressure to compromise, to yield to the status quo. Our answer to the temptations that beguile us, such as cocaine addiction, alcoholism, bigotry and greed, must echo theirs: "Thank you very much, but *no*. We will not bow the knee."

It is interesting that the first challenge Daniel and his three companions faced in Babylon centered around the physical disciplines of diet and appetite. When the man in charge of them wanted them to eat the unclean foods served at King

Nebuchadnezzar's table, Daniel basically said:

> *We would rather not eat what you're eating. The wine looks very tasty, and the king's food looks very rich, but we are under discipline. Test us. Let us eat vegetables and drink water for a time. Then compare our appearance and performance with those of the others.*[10]

Fast So You Will Last

We need to return to the spiritual discipline of Spirit-led fasting to reclaim the true power that comes from walking in the Spirit. I will never forget the counsel an elderly sanctified woman, a seasoned warrior for the Lord, gave me one day: "If you don't fast, you won't last."

Maybe I was naive, but I took her words seriously because I wanted to last. Today, I am blessed with a growing church and the added responsibilities of the bishopric. More than ever before, I want to *last.* I want to live right and live holy before the Lord.

What does it profit me to have all of the outward trappings of success if my soul is empty and my ministry is devoid of true power in the Holy Ghost? I want to live with a perpetual fire in my heart. I want to walk before the Lord in humility and purity so that when I lay my hands on the sick and pray, I will see the Lord move in healing and deliverance. I want ready access to the power and unending creativity of God so I can lead in His strength through continual challenge and change.

There is a growing war against the saints and against every institution that represents righteousness and integrity. If we, as the Church, don't want to waste more seasons, then we must access all of the influence God affords us. We need to seek all of the anointing He offers us, with every ounce of knowledge, wisdom and power available to us through His Word and the Holy Spirit. We need more than one day's supply; we must prepare for the days to come. Then, when confronted with the choice between comfort and compromise, we will be able to confidently say: "It is better for us to die in Christ than to bow down before the world."

If You Say, "Here We Go Again," Then You Won't

Perhaps our greatest danger is familiarity with the fire of God. It seems we are no longer moved by it as we once were. The things of God have become familiar. We are so used to the fragrance of His anointing and the abundance of revelation, knowledge and prophetic words that we tend to roll our eyes and say, "Here we go again," if God sends them too close to our prescheduled Sunday dinner.

The next deadly step is to take the holy things of God for granted. Before you know it, your whole faith system will be compromised. I believe we are approaching an hour of mass deception when many of the elect will be drawn to false saviors *within* the Church. They will appear to have the right pulpit, the right choir and impressive credentials of bishop or apostle; yet something will be amiss in New Jerusalem.

False doctrine and the solicitations of the affections of men are wrong in every generation and culture. Addiction and compulsion have many disguises, fragrances and mannerisms that can easily fool the uninformed and the undiscerning.

The evil spirit of greed, pride and self-exaltation that seduced King Nebuchadnezzar into making the golden image of idolatry has risen up on modern American culture, although the body of Babylon's long-dead king has been in the grave for several thousand years. The purpose of this ancient spirit—to persecute the people of God—is more and more pronounced as we come to the end of the age.

I sense a holy call is summoning the whole Church of God to a season of preparation for persecution. Perhaps it is persecution that causes the Church to be transformed into a ready Bride without spot or wrinkle. In any case, persecution and increased pressure for compromise are sure to come our way in the years ahead. Will we be able and ready to stand firm in our faith? Are we doing so now?

It Will Be Harder for Christians to Fit In

The more secular our society becomes, the more it will become anti-Christian in attitude and policy. It will also become harder and harder for Christians to fit in to American society. We must set our houses in order while continuing to expand, grow and reach out to the lost by faith. The Lord wants us to occupy until He comes, but He also cautioned us to keep on watching, waiting and praying for His return.

Some of the enemy's greatest tools of compromise may be our own friends and family members. If someone close to you consistently pressures you to compromise your faith and your commitment to God, then get yourself away from that person as fast as you can. Run—don't walk—to the nearest place of safety. Break it off; get yourself away from people who want you to bow down to false gods!

Did you know that Jesus said, "Then shall they deliver you up to be afflicted, and shall kill you: and ye shall be hated of all nations for my name's sake"?[11] How many would come forward with that kind of altar call today?

I know this isn't the "shouting material" we like to hear, but it is the prophetic message I hear in my spirit—a message that is reflected in God's Word. Where have all the real leaders gone? Why are the American people so afraid of prophetic leadership and real liberators? Who is the real God of Israel, and is He our God too?

We have lived in the valley of compromise and mediocrity for so long that we tend to kill true liberators and spiritual reformers in the name of preserving the status quo. If we don't do the deed ourselves through backbiting, political intrigue or overt schemes of verbal murder and character assassination, then we allow ourselves to be bought off by more popular and politically correct leaders who promise instant comforts and flatter us, while we turn our heads and they remove or dismiss God's chosen messengers and his bony-fingered prophets.

Public Character Assassinations

We are already seeing people do their duty by destroying ardent public champions of biblical standards through public character assassinations. Those who honor biblical prophecy understand that the day is coming when leaders of political action groups, political parties, special interest groups and the national media will sincerely believe they have done the nation a service when they denounce, limit or even kill "right-wing religious radicals."

All it takes in our supercharged media era is a random, unsubstantiated *rumor* to destroy a lifelong ministry overnight. Those running outreach and rehabilitation programs for children and adolescents seem to be the most vulnerable to "death by rumor." Many people who are convicted by the media and sentenced by public opinion commit suicide or disappear from public life rather than live in unending but undeserved shame. Murder by rumor and death by innuendo is an effective tool in the hands of amoral antagonists.

The best answer to such attacks is godly faith demonstrated through practical works of righteousness. Churches and individual believers across the land are exerting godly influence by meeting human needs and by buying buildings and renovating old businesses in the "bad parts" of their cities. They fulfill the Gospel mandate spiritually and physically by restoring the old, forgotten and fallen things to new life. God's people must take up the challenge to do things that the government and an army of politicians can never do: restore life to the fallen and dying.

Welcome to the Invincible Church

The Church that takes the Gospel of Christ to the lost and reaches out to feed the hungry, clothe and house the homeless, and heal the sick is an invincible Church. Oddly enough, the Church enjoys its finest hour in times and circumstances of persecution. It happened in the Book of Acts, and it happened in the last century when the Church prospered in China and the former USSR despite fierce opposition by the Communists in power.

Got Persecution? Get Prayer

What did the Church in the first century have in common with the churches in Communist China and the former USSR? They *prayed* (but didn't gossip). When officials imprisoned some of the apostles in Jerusalem, the Church responded by calling a prayer meeting and praying, "Lord, behold their threatenings. Now since they are threatening us, give us more power and anointing. Give us more favor and more influence so we can boldly proclaim your name even louder!"[12]

It is time to reclaim the flame of your passion for Christ. Get your song back and dance with joy once again. Consecrate and separate yourself to God all over again, and He will restore your testimony and ignite your holy passion. There is nothing more glorious than a life lived to the limit for Christ.

On the other hand, if you bow down, you become one of

them. If you bow down to the false gods in our world, you lose your uniqueness and squander your special anointing. The favor of man is nothing compared to the favor of God. Hold tight to your integrity. Don't bow! Don't give in! Let them throw you into the flames of human disapproval and public dismissal—God will walk at your side through it all!

When the pressures of compromise come against you, pause for a moment. God's Word says, "Be still, and know that I am God."[13] After this moment of stillness, begin to pray and talk to the One who created you, but do it in faith, trusting Him to hear and answer your prayer.[14]

Then, open your mouth, lift your hands and magnify God. Praise Him, adore Him, lift up His holy name. Praise Him from whom all blessings flow! How do the words go? "Some through the water, some through the flood, some through great trials but all through the blood."

Take the Plunge

We need to let go of the ropes and take the "Jonah plunge." Shout to your circumstances and to hindering limitations ,"Throw me overboard! I've got a hiding place in the Word of God. I have a safe refuge in the midst of my storm; I'll find safety and peace in the Rock of my salvation."

You press through these circumstances and these limitations, by pressing into His presence. Do whatever it takes to find Him. Pray, weep, cry and worship Him all night if necessary. No matter how hot your fire of adversity may be, you can stand fast because your confidence is not in man, but in *"Him who is able."*

No man or devil can take your soul, your joy or your hope, because they cannot take His Name. They cannot touch or withstand His unspeakable power and anointing. No one can take His favor and blessing from you!

We must walk and live in the reality that we are aliens in this world, and citizens of the kingdom of heaven. We can't afford to get too comfortable with the blessings and pleasures of this life. We need to remember that all of it can go tomorrow—tailor-made clothes, rings, suits, cars, houses, social status and, yes, even money. However, God keeps those who refuse to bow and who set their course to stand for Christ at any cost.

— Endnotes ——————————————————————————

1 Dan. 3:12, emphasis mine.

2 Dan. 3:15.

3 Job 13:15a.

4 Dan. 5:12.

5 *The Holman Bible Dictionary* (Nashville: Holman Bible Publishers, 1991); and "PC Bible Atlas for Windows 1.0k, Copyright ©1993, Parsons Technology"; components of "The QuickVerse Library, version 1.0g," Copyright ©1995, 1996 by Craig Rairdin and Parsons Technology, Inc., Hiawatha, IA. From the article "Hananiah."

6 Ibid., from the article "Meshach."

7 Ibid., from the article "Abednego."

8 Ibid., from the article "Belteshazzar." Scholars differ about the exact meaning of this name, but the meaning behind the name of a Babylonian co-regent called King Belshazzar (mentioned in Dan. 5:1) also has various suggested meanings, including "Bel's prince" and "Bel, protect the king."

9 2 Tim. 1:7.

10 My paraphrase of Dan. 1:5–16.

11 Matt. 24:9 KJV. Jesus prophesied these words in the context of what would happen to Jerusalem at the hands of Titus and his Roman legions after He had been resurrected. However, I believe they also apply to the persecution against the Church in the last days.

12 See Acts 4:29–31 for the details of this incredible true story.

13 Ps. 46:10a.

14 Heb. 11:6.

9

Doubt

The strongest chains binding the human race are not made of iron, steel or brass. They are the chains of the soul. These inward shackles, manacles and weighted balls bind our hearts and minds more securely than any physical restraint ever could.

Free men and women who become prisoners of war or land in a jail cell unjustly are still free within. They have the inner resources to soar and escape their physical bonds as long as they are free in mind and spirit. But those who are prisoners within are prisoners indeed, with little hope for the future.

The apostle Paul wrote some of his greatest letters to the Church on parchments bearing the stink of his jail cell. Many other magnificent works of literature, such as John Bunyan's *Pilgrim's Progress,* were penned by free men and women held in the dungeons of governments and the shackles of tyrants.

Jesus Christ totally delivered us from the slavery of sin and religious legalism about two thousand years ago. Since then, He has worked tirelessly to get the slavery and bondage out of the hearts and thinking patterns of each generation. This isn't anything new to God. The Book of Exodus is a record of God's efforts to take the slavery out of the former slaves He delivered from Egyptian bondage.

The Israelites started well at the beginning of their exodus. While the king of Egypt entertained second thoughts about releasing his nation's largest slave population, the Bible says, "The children of Israel went out with boldness [the King James says "with a *high hand*]."¹ Nobody can "gloat" and celebrate a long-awaited victory like former slaves, or like underdogs when they finally whip a bully! That is what the children of Israel did the day they marched out of Rameses loaded down with the gold and precious jewels of their former Egyptian captors.

They Held Their Heads High . . . in the Beginning

Moses, God's chosen deliverer, took stubborn Pharaoh through a series of plagues that devastated Egypt and finally broke his resistance against God's command. When the king of Egypt changed his mind and pursued the children of Israel, they all watched while God miraculously destroyed his army in the waters of the Red Sea.

Then Jacob's descendants began the eleven-day journey from the shores of the Red Sea to the bank of the river Jordan bordering the Promised Land of Canaan. In the beginning, they held their heads high and walked into their destiny with squared shoulders because they realized they were called to be more than slaves. It was time for them to be free.

The crushing weight of slavery had been lifted. They would no longer be limited to being consumers only; God had called them to become entrepreneurs. They would no longer live in rented houses and farm the fields of others; God had called them to possess a land. This time, they wouldn't enter and leave a land as pilgrims; they were its possessors. God had called them to be a prosperous, overcoming, victorious people.

They experienced the supreme power of the God who called them out of slavery in three ways on the day Moses said, "Do not be afraid. Stand still, and see the salvation of the LORD."[2]

First, they *stood still before God in their desperation.*

Second, Moses *stretched out his hand and held the rod of God, and witnessed the miracle-working power of God.* Moses extended the rod of God over the obstacle blocking their path to freedom, and a powerful east wind arose to part the Red Sea. The path was so broad that the entire nation could cross on dry land while the angel of the Lord held Pharaoh's army at bay. When you're not sure what to do, stand still until you hear the voice of the Lord clearly tell you what to do.

Holding Back the Sea

The third step may have been the hardest. The moment came when the children of Israel had to *step into God's provision by faith*—between the walls of water. It was one thing to see God part the waters while standing safely on the shore. It was quite another to step onto the dry seabed and trust Him to hold the watery walls in position long enough for them to pass over. That took courage—and faith. After the children of Israel had passed through the water to the other side, they watched Moses lift the rod again at God's command, and they saw the waters close in and drown Pharaoh's elite army. What do you think they must have felt at that moment?

It is logical to assume that after witnessing so many miracles in Egypt and at the Red Sea, the children of Israel would say, "The Lord our God is able. We can do anything because God is on our side." The problem is that the children of Israel were *real* people like us, and like us, they had a great capacity for doubt, unbelief and forgetfulness.

Once the people reached the borders of Canaan, it was time to survey the land. Moses sent twelve handpicked spies on a mission to examine the Promised Land and report on its inhabitants, geography, crops and foliage, and city fortifications.[3]

When the spies returned, only two of the twelve came back with a faith-filled report; the rest took the negative view of the Promised Land:

> Then Caleb quieted the people before Moses, and said, "Let us go up at once and take possession, for we are well able to overcome it." But the men who had gone up with him said, "We are not able to go up against the people, for they are stronger than we . . . [the] land . . . devours its inhabitants, and all the people whom we saw in it are

men of great stature. There we saw the giants . . . and we were like grasshoppers in our own sight, and so we were in their sight." (Num. 13:30–33)

The Lord Gave the Israelites What They Said

God swiftly responded to these murmurs of doubt and unbelief. The ten men who had brought a negative report immediately died of a plague, and the Lord gave the Israelites what they had declared with their own mouths. No one over the age of twenty was allowed to enter the Promised Land. The Israelites wandered in the wilderness for forty years and died in the desert. Of the older generation, only Joshua and Caleb, along with those who were younger than twenty, crossed the Jordan into Canaan.[4] *Jacob's descendants had trusted God to lead them out of slavery, but they did not trust God to lead them into the Promised Land.*

It is a challenge to get slaves to believe they are really free. Slaves freed during the Civil War in the United States had a difficult time adjusting to their new freedoms. They were used to saying, "Yes sir, no sir; yes ma'am, and no ma'am." And even now, more than one hundred years later, this mental and cultural bondage still clings to many African Americans.

The problem is that slaves are not used to thinking for themselves (that is done for them by others). Slaves are not used to the buying and selling of the business world; slaves are used to being bought and sold. Slaves are not used to owning anything. They

live in borrowed or rented dwellings, or in housing provided by
their owners.

God Abolished Slavery of the Soul

Slaves find it hard to put down roots because they are used to
coming in and going out like migrant workers at the whims of
other people. That is the mentality of slavery and bondage. I
thank God slavery was abolished in our nation many years ago;
but even more, I thank Him for abolishing slavery of the soul
nearly two thousand years ago!

Regardless of your skin color or family background, you are
not a slave anymore; neither am I. Millions of Christians of all
nationalities and ethnic backgrounds needlessly trudge through
life shackled with a deadly slave mentality. They don't realize that
the promises of God always come with challenges. They "try
God's Word once" but give up at the first sign of adversity or
opposition.

My friend, if it's worth having, it's worth fighting for.
Freedom is worth the struggle. Your destiny in Christ is worth
the price it costs to overcome obstacles. I can guarantee you that
there are no easy rides in God's kingdom.

An entire generation of the children of Israel forfeited their
future. They knew God well enough to believe He could lead
them out of slavery, but because of their unbelief, they could not
be led into their rightful destiny. They had the faith to believe
that God wanted them to be delivered, but they failed to stretch

out in faith and believe that He also wanted them to be established in the land He had promised to them.

Their Unbelief Placed a Limit on God's Ability to Bless Them

When God redeemed the first generation of Israelites from slavery, they had to learn how to keep themselves clean, comb their hair and provide for themselves. They were free on the outside but they still felt like slaves on the inside. This affected the way they lived.

In this new millennium I believe God is telling us that we are talking and acting like we are still slaves to sin—even though He delivered us from this bondage. Many of us live in a constant state of guilt because we don't really believe that God could forgive us for the things we've done. Believe it: He can and He has! Christ's blood covered it all at Calvary.

We've been delivered from sin slavery, but we're still living on the devil's plantation in our minds. We have faith enough to believe that God freed us from the power of sin, but we don't have enough faith to *possess the land* He promised us. The "land" is the dream of having your own business that He planted in your heart many years ago. It is the home you've longed to own after renting for fifteen years, or the college degree you've always wanted to earn. Your Promised Land could be the occupation, profession or ministry that reappears in your dreams year after year—because God put it there, in your heart before you were born. Whatever dream God gives you, it will take faith and supernatural provision to possess it, and that isn't a bad thing. It is a guarantee that the only way you'll achieve it is if God is in it.

The dreams and callings of God never depend upon where *we* came from or how much *we* have available in terms of the skills, abilities or resources required. They depend solely on the un-limited resources and favor of God on the one hand and our faith in Him on the other. *Nothing is too difficult for God* as long as we trust Him and deal with the all-important issues of the heart.

God Is the Great Dream-Maker

In the eloquent words of Paul, "For you did not receive the spirit of bondage again to fear, but you received the Spirit of adoption by whom we cry out, 'Abba, Father.'"[5] You must elevate your level of faith and hope. God is the great dream-maker, and He has the power and the will to make His dreams in your life come true. Your part is to believe that He can and will. After all, you are no longer a slave; you are a child of the Almighty God. "The earth is the Lord's, and all its fullness."[6] God just wants to know what you are going to do about it now.

We aren't talking about money or possessions; we are talking about attitude. You can walk through life with your head held low and your eyes on the ground like a slave, or you can lift up your head and watch the King of Glory lead *you* to your Promised Land. The choice—and the consequence of that choice—is all yours.

One of the most irritating phrases in any language shows up in the thirteenth chapter of the Book of Numbers. It was the creed of the "other men" who spied out the land of Canaan with Joshua and Caleb. They said, *"We are not able. . . ."*[7] We are not able? God was sick of hearing that phrase then, and He's sick of hearing it now.

God had a problem because the children of Israel had responded to the negative report. He wanted to take them to another level, but they talked themselves right out of a blessing. Now He wants to take you and me to a new level too; what will He hear us say? Will He hear us say, "We are not able . . ." or, "We can do all things through Christ who strengthens us!"?[8]

They Limited God with Their Own Limits

The first generation of Israelites delivered from Egypt in effect limited God when they reached the limits of their own abilities. They should have realized that *our limits* are nothing more than a boundary marking the point where we hand the baton over to God, the unlimited One.

When you put a limit on God, you also put a limit on your hopes, your possibilities and your potential prosperity. When you put a limit on God, you limit your own inheritance and destiny to a realm *without* God. It forever limits you to what *you can* produce and what you can work up with your own resources. God delivered you from bondage, but if you don't let him take you to the Promised Land, you are saying that you still want to be a slave and you still want to be poor. Don't do it; there is much *more* out there for you in Christ.

The whole earth is the Lord's: He is pouring out blessings and opportunities so great that we can't even contain them. We need to learn how to look and move with God when God opens those doors for us. We don't have time to stop at the river of indecision for a "doubt and unbelief session." We must go forward by faith and follow God into our rightful destiny.

We all need new ways of thinking, ways that honor God and limit our limitations. As usual, God allowed for that ahead of time. His Word declares, "And do not be conformed to this world, but be *transformed by the renewing of your mind,* that you may prove what is that good and acceptable and perfect will of God."[9] The Greek word that is translated here as "renewing" literally means "renovating."[10] So if you ever had any doubts, put them now to rest: you are experiencing a complete "mind renovation" at the moment.

Never Put Human Limits
Ahead of the Power of Unlimited Divinity

Our "failures at the river Jordan" don't happen all at once; they are the end result of a process. The Israelites put a limit on God *after* they went out of Egypt with boldness. They began the journey well, but the farther into the dry wilderness they went, the weaker they became. The closer they came to the Promised Land, the more they felt their weariness and frustration. This seems to be a general principle: the closer you get to a divine promise, the greater becomes your weariness.

Finally the Israelites put their own human limits ahead of God's unlimited divinity. They limited God with their declarations of doubt and unbelief. They were saying, "God, You are challenging and pushing us too far. You are stretching us too much, and we don't like it. Let us go back to the ease of slavery where everything was handed to us and we were never stretched."

Do you remember the teachers who stretched you the most in school? Some of them wore glasses and had beady eyes that you just couldn't avoid or put off. There was something about the way they pushed and probed at you that forced you to become more than you thought you could be. They prodded you to do more than you thought could be done.

I recently fell into the hands of a member of my congregation who had that same gift for stretching others. This brother said the Lord had led him to "help me work out" at the local gym. Secretly, I didn't want to believe it was God—surely, I thought, this brother just wanted to get back at me for a message I had preached.

I Chose Comfort; He Chose Difficulty

But for some reason I agreed to go with him to the gym. And when we were there, we went to the bench press. I selected a weight I knew I could handle comfortably. That wasn't good enough for this brother. He insisted on adding just enough weight to make things difficult for his pastor (he only had my best interest at heart, of course).

While I squirmed to find just the right position for my feat of strength, he stayed right by me in case I lost control of the increased load. Then he stepped into his true "stretching" anointing. "Okay, come on, Bishop," he said. "You've got to push, Bishop! Push that bar in the Name of Jesus; push!" At that moment, everything in me wanted to jump off that bench and remind him, "Young man, this is your bishop you are humiliating here."

My new weight-training mentor put his little finger under the bar while I struggled mightily under the load. I really thought I was doing all the work until he removed his finger. Then the bar seemed to double its weight in a matter of seconds, and I became very irritated. (He hadn't done anything wrong; it was my embarrassment talking.) I told him, "Now if this is going to work, we need to remember that I am the pastor, and you are the member."

His gentle answer was both proper and profound. He said, "Bishop, in this environment, I am in charge." I just looked at him and said, "Take me to the next weight, son." I didn't like it at the moment, because it challenged me to go to a level that I had not mastered. However, it didn't take long for me to appreciate my instructor's persistent pushing, especially when I started seeing improvement in my strength and build. This didn't happen because he let me stay comfortable; it happened because he pushed me.

Do You Have the Limitless Kind of Faith?

God wants to birth a limitless kind of faith in our lives because He is a limitless God who always desires more for us than we want for ourselves. He challenges us daily to look beyond the so-called facts and make a leap of faith in Jesus' name. This is the essence of what Jesus was saying when He told His disciples, "If anyone desires to come after Me, let him deny himself, and take up his cross daily, and follow Me."[11]

The earth was not created with facts; it was created by the creative Word of God. The stars, the moon and the sun were hung in space at the Word of the Lord. Facts are useful, and the Lord gave us logical minds and inquiring intellects to accumulate facts and utilize them in our quest for knowledge. However, the God of creation never wanted us to worship facts and intellectual pursuits as "god" in His place. He always reserves the right to transcend the laws of nature and matter when it suits His purposes.

When you want to purchase a home, you need *faith* before you need money. When you look in the newspaper for a job, a business opportunity or something you need, do it by faith and God will meet your faith and activate His promises on your behalf. Go to the bank and seek a loan by faith so that God can meet you at the point of your faith. When you enroll your son and your daughter in college, do it by faith. Stop telling your children, "Well, I don't have the money to send you and your brother to school"—that's just another version of saying, "We are not able. . . ." God does not want to hear that. He wants you to claim your rightful destiny.

Stretch Out on His Word; Reach for the Stars on His Promises

God wants to do more than take us out of bondage. He wants to take us in to possess the land! God wants us to stretch out on His Word and reach out for the stars on the strength of His faithfulness and glory. Step outside of the circle of your limitations and plant your feet on the foundation of His eternal promises. Dare to do something you have never done before. Trust God and step out; and watch God work a miracle for you.

What is God's will for your life? The answer is in His Word: "Beloved, I pray that you may prosper in all things and be in health, just as your soul prospers."[12] When Moses looked out over the Red Sea and wondered what to do next, the Lord told him, "Stop crying. What's in your hand? *Now stretch it out!*"[13]

Everything God gave you is in your hand—your gifts, talents, abilities and all of the resources at your disposal. Stretch out your hand like Moses: everything you need to part the water and pass over to the Promised Land is in your hand. Plant your feet, clear your throat, extend your hand and speak God's purposes for your life into existence. The New International Bible translates Proverbs 16:3 this way: "Commit to the Lord whatever you do, and your plans will succeed."

Fuel your dreams and the dreams of your children with the

Word of God and the power of the Holy Spirit. It's not too late. God gives us dreams and goals to help us step beyond our limitations and trust Him at His Word. So take a leap of faith, step out into "nothing" and watch God work a miracle. In the end, He will receive all of the glory—and you will be blessed.

— Endnotes

1. Ex. 14:8b.

2. Ex. 14:13b.

3. Num. 13:17–20.

4. Num. 14.

5. Rom. 8:15.

6. 1 Cor. 10:28.

7. Num. 13:31a, italics mine.

8. Adapted and personalized from Paul's faith declaration in Phil. 4:13.

9. Rom. 12:2, italics mine.

10. James Strong, *Strong's Exhaustive Concordance of the Bible* (Peabody, MA: Hendrickson Publishers, n.d.); meanings and definitions drawn from the word derivations for **renewed** (Greek, #342, *"anakainosis"*).

11. Luke 9:23.

12. 3 John 2.

13. Ex. 14:15–16, emphasis mine.

10

Finances

The pastor prayed solemnly over the Sunday offering just as the offering plates began to crisscross the pews. Everyone had their checks written and properly sealed in their offering envelopes when the pastor added, "Dear Lord, no matter what we say or do, this is what we think of You. Amen."

Imagine the silent shock wave that hit that group of people dressed in their Sunday best. Suddenly a new perspective of monetary gifts to the Invisible God dawned on hundreds of hearts and minds—with gripping conviction!

Now put yourself in that position for a moment. Faced with those words, how many of us would feel a sudden impulse to retrieve our sealed offering envelope and insert a drastically different gift for the Lord? It is a sobering thought.

One day Jesus Christ did something even more shocking. He used four short sentences to unravel all of man's pompous ideas about human generosity and unveiled God's true viewpoint on *maximum investment.* And in so doing, he instantly rendered obsolete every man-made monetary and economic theory for individuals, groups and even nations.

The Lord's words at the temple in Jerusalem forever changed our concept of giving gifts to God. He launched His missile with a summons and a nod as He spoke of a poor widow:

> *Now Jesus sat opposite the treasury and saw how the people put money into the treasury. And many who were rich put in much. Then one poor widow came and threw in two mites, which make a quadrans. So He called His disciples to Himself and said to them, "Assuredly, I say to you that this poor widow has put in more than all those who have given to the treasury; for they all put in out of their abundance, but she out of her poverty put in all that she had, her whole livelihood." (Mark 12:41–44)*

This widow and her two copper coins occupy only four lines in the Gospels of Mark and Luke, and those two coins were the equivalent of only one-eighth of a cent. That sure doesn't amount to much, but something compels us to talk about that widow and her two little coins two thousand years later!

This was an era in human history when women were generally considered to be of less value than men in virtually every major culture (but not in the eyes of Jesus Christ). In fact, females were often viewed more as property or objects than as individual human beings created in God's image. In many cases, they were considered to be a great expense, not an asset. I am told the Communist government of China embraces a similar value system today. As a matter of official policy, Chinese physicians are forced to abort many female children every year.

Jewish fathers viewed female children who failed to find a husband as little more than a lifelong responsibility and financial burden. Women did not enjoy the same social or economic status as men in that day; so Jesus Christ was revolutionizing religious and social thought when He helped us understand, through Paul, that "there is neither Jew nor Greek, there is neither slave nor free, *there is neither male nor female; for you are all one in Christ Jesus.*"[1]

Widows Without Sons
Often Begged on the Streets

In ancient Jewish culture, a young woman was the property of her father until ownership or "title" was transferred to her husband. If her husband died, her only hope was to have sons who could assume ownership over her and provide for her needs. For this reason, it was common for widows with no sons or other male relatives to live in abject poverty, with some being forced to beg on the streets for survival.

Social Security didn't exist then, and there were no welfare offices. As far as I am aware, no one in Israel collected benevolent offerings to sustain homeless widows until the first Christian church was established in Jerusalem. It is not surprising, therefore, that most widows were poor.

Most of us assume that this is a wonderful but *dated* Bible story. The temple no longer exists, and times have changed an awful lot since that incident nearly two thousand years ago. But truthfully, *I think Jesus still watches us while we give,* and I suspect He does it with the same keen perception He demonstrated at the temple treasury.

God knows what we give and how we give it. That means He knows our attitudes and every nuance of the nonverbal communication we broadcast to Him and to the people around us when we give. And how we give determines where—and from whom—we will receive recognition and blessing![2]

God Is More Interested in Our Leftovers Than in Our Gifts

Frankly, more of us ought to be concerned about the Lord's response to our acts of giving. I want the same response the Lord gave to this widow's offering after she put in all she had!

God is more concerned with "what we have left over" than with what we actually put into the offering plate. He is also concerned with the amount of time we invest in prayer, and with the way we treat the poor, the widowed and the fatherless. The principle behind it all is straight and it is the antithesis of hell: "Little becomes much when we put it in the Master's hand."

Jesus was unimpressed with the grand gifts given by the rich and the powerful. He knew it was nothing for them to make such large contributions. Those who are wealthy should remember the principle David revealed when he refused to offer God something that cost him nothing. He said, "I will surely buy it for the full price, for I will not . . . offer burnt offerings with *that which costs me nothing.*"[3]

The Lord pointed to the lowly widow who gave less than a penny to God and publicly praised her, saying, "Assuredly, I say to you that this poor widow has put in more than all those. . . ."[4] The way we give says something about who we are and what we value the most.

An Example of Righteous Giving

This destitute widow gave everything she had to God. She leaned on Him as her only hope, not knowing that God the Son would see her act of faith and make her an eternal example of righteous giving for His kingdom. This widow gave her gift "out of her poverty." The meaning of the Greek word translated as "poverty" here is stronger than our word "poverty" implies. It should be translated as "penury" or "*extreme* poverty."[5]

Did you notice that even though this woman was poor, she didn't "give poor"? She was poor through no choice of her own, but she gave richly by choice, through faith. The poor widow gave richly because she was determined to be included in the offering. She did not have much, but she gave all that she had because she was rich in faith.

By international standards, most of us would be considered wealthy; yet we give poorly. We often give poorly because we are poor in faith, prayer, worship and in the quality and depth of our commitments to God and one another. This woman put all of her trust in God and backed it up with an all-out investment in Him and in His Word. That is why we are talking about her today, instead of the wealthy religious people who poured bags of gold into the treasury.

God isn't concerned with the money; He owns the cattle on the thousand hills and all of the gold, silver, diamonds and other resources buried under those hills.[6] The Bible says, "For the Lord does not see as man sees; for man looks at the outward appearance, but the Lord looks at the heart."[7] In fact, right after He pointed out the widow who gave two mites, Jesus prophesied that the grand temple in Jerusalem, with all of its gold, silver and fine inlaid gems, would be torn down stone by stone—and it happened exactly as He said it would.[8]

Your Attitude Determines Your Perspective

If you have a grudging attitude toward "paying" your tithe and offerings, then your perspective of giving is that you *have to do it.* The widow Jesus pointed out had a joyful, hopeful attitude of faith, and she *wanted to be included* in the worship of giving to God. She was trying to be honest. "I don't have what other people have, and I can't give like some people give, but my faith is strong because I know that God is in charge. I own nothing, so I will give to Him out of my poverty."

This widow was authentic and genuine when she *worshipped*

God with her giving. It did not matter to her what other people thought about her gift; only God's opinion counts. Jesus praised the attitude of her heart. Her attitude supernaturally multiplied the eternal value of her meager monetary gift. Jesus made it a point to contrast the widow's gift with those of others: "Assuredly, I say to you that this poor widow *has put in more than all those* who have given to the treasury; *for they all put in out of their abundance,* but she *out of her poverty put in all that she had,* her whole livelihood."[9] It was this woman's attitude that made her giving outshine all of the extravagant gifts other people gave to the Lord.

What is your attitude doing to the gifts you give to God? Paul told the Philippians:

> *Indeed I have all and abound. I am full, having received from Epaphroditus the things sent from you, a sweet-smelling aroma, an acceptable sacrifice, well pleasing to God. And my God shall supply all your need according to His riches in glory by Christ Jesus. (Phil. 4:18–19)*

Offer Acceptable Sacrifices;
Then Claim the Reward

We like to jump past the first verse and "stand" on the promise in the second verse. It doesn't work, of course; God can't honor our claim that He will supply all of our need according to His riches in glory until we *obediently* give Him a fragrant and acceptable sacrifice of our finances, our time and our talents.

The reward for the widow's mites came only after the widow had offered her *all*. She gave what she had, and in doing so she pleased God. I doubt that Jesus was the only one who noticed her. She probably had more than her share of critics telling her, "Woman, stop that. Why would you give the temple your last mites? After all, what is God going to do with two measly mites? It doesn't make sense! Why would you even try?"

Some of her acquaintances probably saw her "throw away" the last coins in her possession and wondered if she had lost her mind, but that was because they didn't understand the economy of God. Faith is the rare and priceless commodity of heaven; gold is merely road-building material. Giving is more sacrificial than sensible and it is more supernatural than natural.

A "sensible god" would never send His only begotten Son to die so we could live. That is the act of our all-wise, all-knowing God of love and mercy, but it could never be called "sensible." A sensible god would remember what we give; but our God records what we keep.

Do You Possess Your Possessions or Do They Possess You?

Too many of us are bound by and addicted to our possessions. Paul the apostle said, "Moreover it is required in stewards that one be found faithful."[10] God is not as concerned with what we are holding as with what is holding us. In a very real sense, none of us really owns anything. It is God who gives us power to get wealth. (He possesses the gifts, the good health, the creative ideas and the divine favor that pave the road to success in business, on the job, in the ministry and in our service to others.)[11] According to the Book of Psalms, God gets pleasure from prospering His people.[12] We don't own anything; we are only *stewards* of what has been given and entrusted to us. Even our days on the earth and the breath in our lungs are gifts from God, for which we will be held accountable.

As the old folk used to say, "God has allowed us to have good jobs and to receive a decent salary." The whole earth is *still* the Lord's. According to the Bible, that includes "all its fullness, the world and those who dwell therein."[13] If we acknowledge God owns everything, then that should change the way we serve and give.

We don't have to "guess" about God's feelings or plan for our lives. His Word says, "Beloved, I pray that you may prosper in all things and be in health, just as your soul prospers."[14] I am praying that our children will capture this nugget of truth even if our generation fails to pass the test. I hope our children will see and understand how much God has invested in us so He can "establish His covenant" in the earth.[15]

How many times have you heard people say, "I'm going to start giving back to God as soon as I get that big inheritance check, or as soon as I get that bonus I deserve"? The problem is that if you can't be faithful to give a monthly tithe and offering from the $200 or $2,000 you receive now, how will you manage to give 10 or 15 percent of $3,000 or $10,000 each month? It won't happen.

What Do You Have Left
after You Give Him Your Gift?

God is watching us. He wants to see what we have left after we give Him what we feel "He has coming." Jesus looked at the widow and commended her for her faithfulness to give, even out of her lack. She wanted to acknowledge that her God had been good to her, and that pleased Him. She was not possessed by her possessions; she was possessed by her love for God and her desire to honor Him.[16]

Too many of us try to "ride into prosperity on someone else's coattail." Like the relatives who "come out of the woodwork" when someone receives a large sum of money, some of us hope to get caught up in someone else's blessing and favor. Never expect to reap the benefits of another person's blessings without doing your part of the work.

> *Because of laziness the building decays, and through idleness of hands the house leaks. A feast is made for laughter, and wine makes merry; but money answers everything. (Eccles. 10:18–19)*

We can't be lazy and still expect the windows of heaven to open for us. God watches how we give to Him, whether we do it in secret or in the open. In the parable of the talents, Jesus made it clear that He holds us personally responsible for the way we handle His gifts and blessings in this life.

Will You Stake Your Future on God's Faithfulness?

The widow gave what she had to God and trusted Him to support her and preserve her life. She looked to Him as her kinsman-redeemer, and she staked her future on God's faithfulness. Can you do the same? That is God's will for each of us.

Solomon said, "Cast your bread upon the waters, for you will find it after many days."[17] Take the gifts God has given you and dare to cast them out upon the waters of His faithfulness. Step out by faith and use what He has given you for His glory and good pleasure.

The Book of Proverbs is essentially a book about the fruit of attitudes. Here are three verses that focus on the contrast between a liberal or generous heart and a selfish heart:

> *There is one who scatters, yet increases more; and there is one who withholds more than is right, but it leads to poverty. The generous soul will be made rich, and he who waters will also be watered himself. The people will curse him who withholds grain, but blessing will be on the head of him who sells it. (Prov. 11:24–26)*

Do you generously scatter (or invest) your gifts and resources by faith in people and Spirit-led ministries and watch them increase? Or do you withhold your tithes, offerings, talents and time from the Kingdom because you "can't afford to give them away"? (You will probably see them dwindle away anyway.) Doesn't this sound a great deal like an Old Testament version of the parable of the talents?

The Kingdom Economy
Runs Contrary to the World's Economy

God's Word never contradicts itself. The economy of the Kingdom runs contrary to the financial principles of the world. God says, "Give, and it will be given to you: good measure, pressed down, shaken together and running over will be put into your bosom. For with the same measure that you use, it will be measured back to you."[18] In another place, the Bible says, "The generous soul will be made rich, and he who waters will also be watered himself."[19]

The widow at the temple treasury could have reasoned, "I don't have much to give, and it would make more sense for me to hold on to what I have." But we know from Jesus' observation that she chose the path of faith instead of doubt and unbelief. She may have said to herself, "I could hold back what little I have, but I owe God some sign of my gratitude for all He has done for me. I'll give Him back everything He has given to me. I want to make sure that I am numbered among the faithful and the thankful."

The widow who gave two mites to God had the highest of all motives: she wanted to please God. What motives does God see in your heart when the offering plate passes by? You and I can receive the same approval from God that this precious widow received. All it takes is a pure heart, a right attitude about giving and a heartfelt desire to please God above all things.

The pure-heart motive to make your maximum investment in our "Maximum God" will lead you into greater faith, purer love and sweeter communion with God. God delights to use and bless people who long to please Him more than they want the approval and praise of men.

We need to ask ourselves the question recorded in Psalm 116:12: "What shall I render to the Lord for all His benefits toward me?"

I am sure that poor widow asked herself that question before she made her way to the temple that day:

What can I give the Lord today? I don't have much but want to give Him something!

I am breathing, and the good Lord woke me up this morning and graciously gave me another day of life. I must give Him something precious in appreciation for His precious gift of life.

I owe Him. I would not be alive today had it not been for the Lord on my side. . . . All I have are two mites—I will give Him that. Yes, I will give Him all that I have, for it came from His hand anyway.

Sometimes the best way to press through life's pressure points is to give your way out of poverty. It isn't the gift that matters to God; it is the attitude of gratitude in your heart that releases His immeasurable blessings in your life.

— Endnotes

1 Gal. 3:28, italics mine.

2 The Lord taught that people who flaunt their giving of tithes and offerings to impress men limit their reward to the flattery of men. On the other

hand, God openly rewards those who "don't let the left hand know what the right hand is doing" and give secretly to Him (see Matt. 6:1–4).

3   1 Chron. 21:24.

4   Mark 12:43b.

5   James Strong, *Strong's Exhaustive Concordance of the Bible* (Peabody, MA: Hendrickson Publishers, n.d.); meanings and definitions drawn from the word derivations for **poverty** (Greek, #5304, 5302; *"husteresis"*).

6   Ps. 50:10.

7   1 Sam. 16:7b.

8   Mark 13:2; Luke 21:6.

9   Mark 12:43b–44, italics mine.

10 1 Cor. 4:2.

11 Deut. 8:18.

12 Paraphrased from Ps. 35:27b.

13 Ps. 24:1b.

14 3 John 2.

15 Deut. 8:18.

16 Sometimes you cannot tell people what you're doing. During a ministry staff meeting in Atlanta, Georgia, we were surprised to discover that an "extra" $30,000 had been added to the church's finances in the form of a stock investment. Most of the people in the meeting thought that it was just an accounting mistake, but I suggested that it might be a miracle. Later that year, the person administrating the account confirmed that a couple in our congregation had donated the gift after they received a miracle from the Lord. They wanted to give something back to God in gratitude for His gift to them, but they wanted to do it anonymously (and I made sure it remained that way). I knew this couple didn't have that kind of money, but when a miracle came their way, they responded with the generosity of people who really appreciate God's faithfulness and abundant gifts.

17 Eccles. 11:1.

18 Luke 6:38.

19 Prov. 11:25.

11

He Is Still My Shepherd

*But when He saw the multitudes, He was moved with compassion
for them, because they were weary and scattered, like sheep having no
shepherd. (Matt. 9:36)*

In postmodern America, Christians and non-Christians alike
often seem weary and scattered "like sheep having no shepherd."
Inundated with a culture that worships prosperity and material-
ism on the one hand, they feel surrounded by stresses on the
other. Many if not most of us scratch our heads each week and
wonder how we survived in our right minds because these
stresses possess the potential to quickly overwhelm body, soul
and mind.

As noted earlier, the stresses of our overly busy lives come on
fast and furious. Many times we get hit with several stress points
at one time. Something strange happens with the money; peculiar symptoms show up in your body; your children begin to fail
in school; your marriage hits a prolonged bumpy stretch; you

lose a large sum of money in the stock market and then you find out that your job is in jeopardy.

We all know the peculiar signature and imprint of stress on our lives, but do we know the healing balm of the Shepherd of our lives? The greatest cure for what ails us is not found in a self-help program, a medical research center or the latest psychological or psychiatric journals. We find relief not in a thing, but in a Person.

No one said it better than David, the psalmist of old, who was intimately acquainted with the pain of human weakness and the suffocating weight of multiplied sorrows. It was David, the shepherd king, the repentant adulterer and self-confessed murderer, the ultimate worshipper and fear warrior, who described our Cure in the six brief verses of his Twenty-third Psalm:

> *The LORD is my shepherd; I shall not want. He makes me to lie down in green pastures; He leads me beside the still waters. He restores my soul; He leads me in the paths of righteousness For His name's sake. Yea, though I walk through the valley of the shadow of death, I will fear no evil; for You are with me; Your rod and Your staff, they comfort me. You prepare a table before me in the presence of my enemies; You anoint my head with oil; my cup runs over. Surely goodness and mercy shall follow me all the days of my life; and I will dwell in the house of the LORD forever. (Ps. 23:1–6)*

If It Were Not for the Lord . . .

My friend, we must make up our minds and speak it out in desperate times: "No matter what comes my way each new day, the Lord is still my Shepherd."

I know what it is like to minister to grieving family members at a funeral home in one hour, only to enter the pediatric intensive care ward the next hour to bring hope to the hopeless and consolation to the inconsolable. "If it were not for the Lord . . ." The Scripture says, "Through the Lord's mercies we are not consumed, because His compassions fail not."[1] Those of us who have weathered the storms of life recognize the intensity of the stress upon us, and we have sense enough to know that having survived, "everything that hath breath ought to praise Him." We have no need to be pumped up or primed before we praise Him who has saved and delivered us from destruction.

It is during the peculiarly stressful seasons that the familiar foundations of our forefathers in faith come back to us. Unfortunately, some of us have tossed out that which is familiar (the holy) and have chosen the needless over the needful in our zeal for "progress" and "open-mindedness."

This Twenty-third Psalm is one of those "Yes, I know" Scripture passages that suffer from our easy dismissal of the familiar. I preached to my congregation on this passage during a period when we had buried two children, and when two mothers under the age of fifty-six hovered between life and death, waiting for miracles. The three-month-old baby of another mother in our congregation had fallen out of her arms onto her kitchen floor and suffered serious brain injury. Finally, yet another church member suffered a debilitating brain stroke. Yet, in the midst of it all, God was still worthy of all praise because *the Lord is still our Shepherd!*

The Holy Ghost Wouldn't Let Me Turn Away

It is easy in such trying times to be inundated and overcome by what you see and hear. I often go from hospital to hospital on my visitation rounds, but visitation during that period was rougher than most. One day, I visited the pediatric ward to pray for the baby with severe brain injuries. I did my best not to look at the children in the other beds because I knew I couldn't take the emotional pressure of my compassion for them. The Holy Ghost, however, would have none of that. He drew my heart to little children battling with cancer and strokes, and I found myself stopping in room after room to pray for those little ones in the mighty name of Jesus.

Some people just can't help themselves. It is hard for people to be quiet once they have been delivered from physical death. They run the aisles and "disrupt" church services Sunday after Sunday because they know what it is like to be admitted to a hospital wondering if they will ever leave those antiseptic halls alive.

Sometimes they make noise, jerk, collapse on the floor and cry. If you want to understand why, visit the nearest hospital. These people discovered what David meant when he said, "Yea, though I walk through the valley of the shadow of death, I will fear no evil; for You are with me; Your rod and Your staff, they comfort me."[2]

Praise Him in a New Way

I've noticed that this kind of thanksgiving is not confined to Pentecostal people. Once we discover that the Lord is still our Shepherd, we praise Him in a new way, whether we are Catholic, Episcopalian, Presbyterian, Methodist, Baptist or the Church of Christ. It is no accident that Jesus used the sheepfold as a tool to teach us about Himself:

> *The thief does not come except to steal, and to kill, and to destroy. I have come that they may have life, and that they may have it more abundantly. I am the good shepherd. The good shepherd gives His life for the sheep. But a hireling, he who is not the shepherd, one who does not own the sheep, sees the wolf coming and leaves the sheep and flees; and the wolf catches the sheep and scatters them. The hireling flees because he is a hireling and does not care about the sheep. I am the good shepherd; and I know My sheep, and am known by My own.* (John 10:10–14)

The apostle Peter described himself as a "shepherd of the flock of God" and Jesus Christ as "the Chief Shepherd."[3] King David was a shepherd of sheep long before he became a king over men. He was always a shepherd at heart. He also described God as a caring shepherd and a dependable guide. It is clear that God moved in David's life using those childhood experiences with the sheep.

The Qualities of True Followers

David knew what it was like to tend sheep, and like any good shepherd, he knew the nature of sheep. Sheep are completely dependent on their shepherd for provision, guidance and protection. David's Twenty-third Psalm focuses not so much upon the characteristics of sheep as upon the qualities of those who follow Him. "The Lord is *my* shepherd. . . ."

The Creator designed us for divine purpose, unlimited possibility and eternal promise. We often fail because we don't know how to follow the under-shepherd God gives us, just as we fail to follow the Chief Shepherd. I've noticed that many people today don't want anything to do with authority. They don't want to submit to authority of any kind, nor do they want to wield authority, with all of its responsibilities and liabilities.

We must overcome this problem, because authority—the leading, guiding, providing and protecting functions of leadership—must be in our lives if we are to succeed. Flocks composed of sheep that want to shepherd themselves are doomed to destruction. If we can grasp the fact that Jesus is still our Shepherd and follow Him, then we can have more successes than failures in life.

We will be able to lay our heads down at night and go to sleep without medication. Peace will rule in our homes and we won't worry about our children, because we will know Jesus is still our Shepherd. When David said, "He leads me," he was talking about the *present,* not the past. Those who refuse to be led by the unchanging God find themselves at the mercy of their ever-changing circumstances and problems.

Some of us are still fighting our childhood memories. A woman tries to prove to her mother—who died in 1969—that even though she was fast as a teenager, she has become a respectable, loving wife and mother today. A man drives himself to earn nine college degrees and establish fifteen successful businesses, yet he is totally alone, neurotic and psychotic in the extreme. Why? The Lord is not "fueling" these desperate lives. All of their effort and human achievement is driven by the compulsion to overcome a bad memory or cover a "hole" in their personalities that only God can fill.

What Fuels You? Who Leads You?

David knew his Shepherd; do you? What fuels you? Who leads you? We all need to "pause for station identification" and clearly establish who is leading us. A shepherd guides, provides direction, covers and nurtures the sheep. He is dependable, faithful and diligent to watch the sheep in the flock of God. God created us to follow Jesus Christ, not our anger, the past, our drive to compete or our river of weakness. When the Lord leads and inspires us, we don't have to want or worry.

Jesus put it this way: "But seek first the kingdom of God and His righteousness, and all these things shall be added to you."[4] That means, "Seek Him and be holy first; then your needs will be met." Wherever God leads, He feeds. If He is not feeding, then perhaps you should make sure you are walking where He is leading.

Every believer goes through lean seasons that challenge their faith and trust in God, but He supplies our needs. I've learned that I don't have time to worry because "my times" are in His hand.[5] When you give your life to God, He obligates Himself to cover, protect and provide for you. If the Lord is your Shepherd, then you don't have time to worry. You can rest and find contentment and peace of mind in His presence because He is still your Shepherd.

The Greeks Described Time in Four Ways

The English language has one word for what we call "time," but in Greek, there are at least four nouns used to describe time. *Hora* refers to a "season" or recurring time in nature, such as a planting season or the former and latter rains in Israel. This word is still used to refer to "hour" in the Spanish language. *Aion* refers to eternity, or "forever."[6] *Kairos* refers to a set time, a destined, preappointed event in life, and what we might call a window of oppportunity.[7] That means there are some things in our lives that are yet to be established. God has a plan for both your life and mine. It is never too late to seek God's will for your life. In other words, it isn't over until it's over. And *chronos* refers to "a space of time," or a measurement of passing time. This Greek word still shows up in the English words chronology, chronometer, chronograph and chronic. When "chronos time" hooks up with "kairos time," it is God's time for a miracle. I don't have time to waste because I have an appointment with destiny. I have an appointment with possibility and divine promise.

The Good Shepherd constantly demonstrates His love for us by "making us lay down in green pastures." By nature, I am a type A personality to the third degree. I am driven to constantly work, produce and strive for perfection. I love work (I have had jobs since I was thirteen years old). And my mind is always working, even when I'm lying down. The supernatural anointing of the Holy Ghost only accelerates the process.

It is clear to me that I got all this from my father. He would come home after a full day of work at the post office and install all of the cabinets for a kitchen and call it "relaxing." This wasn't normal, and he died of a heart attack at the age of fifty-three. I thank God for my father, but I don't want to go out that way. I am grateful that when I was pushing myself physically to the point of danger, the Lord gave me this warning: "Slow down and stop before you hit a wall."

You Must Be "Unmade" to Be "Remade"

Yes, the Lord made me slow down and get some rest. Through that experience I learned that some of us have to be "unmade" so we can be "remade." It reminds me of the way a parent tells a

child, "Go make your bed." A child will just naturally go for the
"shortcut" method and make the bed by throwing the top quilt
over the whole bed, lumps and all. Most parents would look at
that mess and say, "You get back here and *unmake* the whole
thing! Pull off the comforter, strip back the flannel blanket and
top sheet and fix that fitted sheet on the mattress. Now remake
your bed, layer by layer."

God requires the same of us moment by moment, day by day
and situation by situation. We must be unmade before we can be
made. When God says lay down, that means He intends to
unravel and strip away some lumpy areas hidden under the top
cover of our lives so He can make us over again. The Lord makes
us lay down so He can renew us, re-create us and restore our souls.

The Lord wants us to get our sleep for some very practical reasons. He wants us to rest and reflect on where we've been so we'll
be ready for where we will be going. When was the last time you
had a good nap? Sleep resembles death in several important
ways. Most pastors think the local church would stop if they
died. Yet each night when they fall asleep, the Church goes on
without them. We need sleep just to let us know that we aren't
all that we think we are. The world still turns even though you
stop long enough to get a nap.

Stop and Take Your Rest Now

If you doubt that your body must be replenished and restored,
try going without sleep for two days. Sleep lets you know that

everyone can do without you. When you die and wake up in the arms of Jesus, life on earth will continue without you; so you might as well stop and take your rest right now.

I heard Bishop Ellis tell the story of a young woman who delivered a hard-hitting message that carried wisdom far beyond her physical age. She said, "My message is this: 'Go somewhere and sit down.'" That is a good word: "Go somewhere and sit down. You're getting on everyone else's nerves, so let God make you lie down so you can get your rest."

David said of the Lord, "He restores my soul." Rest is a good thing. Yesterday is history; tomorrow is a mystery; all we really have is the gift of today—that is why they call it a present. There are five ways to be renewed:

1. **Let go of past defeats.** Let them go and get on with life.
2. **Learn to embrace change.** Change is here to stay, but many of us insist on fighting change at any cost. Change never wins a 100 percent approval rating, and if you ever become a leader, you should understand that change upsets people. It doesn't matter: where there is life, there is always change.
3. **Associate with people who are going somewhere.** Seek out godly people who have a sense of God-given purpose and destiny. According to the Book of Proverbs, "He who walks with wise men will be wise, but the companion of fools will be destroyed."[8] Carefully choose leaders who will lead you closer to God and deeper into your destiny. If they

don't have anything to demonstrate the validity of their faith, if they are broke, busted and disgusted, then sooner or later you will bear the same fruit. Beware of people and leaders who encourage you to be less than you can be in Christ. Good leaders always want more for their followers than they want for themselves.

4. **Live to rejoice today.** The Scriptures say, "This is the day the LORD has made; we will rejoice and be glad in it."[9] If the people of God (you and I) really rejoice in each new day the Lord makes, we will have happier churches.

5. **Lighten up.** Don't be so serious all the time. Learn how to laugh and play with childlike joy once more. Enjoy a good clean joke and rejoice in the warmth of sunshine. We need to lighten up, cheer up and live in the sunshine.

David said the Lord always leads His sheep "beside still waters." Sheep are skittish around moving water, perhaps because they can easily drown in troubled waters. I've noticed that I learn and receive guidance most clearly during seasons of stillness before God.

Because He Lives, Fear Has No Hold on Tomorrow

Lie down, be still, rest and reflect on the greatness of God until He renews and re-creates you. Fear loses its stranglehold on your future when you perceive that because *He* lives, you can overcome every obstacle; you "can do all things through Christ who strengthens you."[10]

Many Christians long to be restored, but we scurry from excitement to excitement and from service to service, seeking one experience after another. We aren't restored because we never pause enough to reflect on what the Lord has *already* done. The Bible, and the New Testament in particular, speaks a great deal about the importance of meditation, or inward reflection, and a deep thoughtful consideration of God's Word. If you take time to meditate and reflect, you will discover that, in the meantime, He has restored your soul so you can fulfill your destiny. Reflection and meditation reassure us that our invisible God and King is real, and that He is still seated on the throne.

The Lord our Shepherd makes us to lie down so that we can get to know the God of the sheep. Too many of us are "in the Church" but we're not "in God." We know the protocols and practices of the Church: we know how to bow, we know how to sing the favorite songs and hymns; we know there are sixty-six books in the Bible and we know the appointed "wardrobe" standards of our local church—*but do we know God?* It is not enough to know the address of the sheepfold; we must know the Chief Shepherd.

The true Shepherd leads His flock to green pastures to give them pure nourishment. He shuns the dead overgrowth from last year's experiences. It isn't enough for spiritual sheep to limit their diet to what Mamma said or to the favorite messages of the late Reverend Righteous some twenty-five years ago.

Are You Secure in Religion or in the Living God?

One of the great tragedies of the Church is that our church buildings are filled with religious people who have a secure grip on religion, but they've never secured a genuine relationship with the living God. They serve "the God Mamma served" instead of the God who personally transformed their lives.

Many of our churches are void of power and authority because they put more emphasis on tradition than upon the Word of God. In a sense, we have become an "illustrated sermon" demonstrating the truth of Hosea 4:6: "My people are destroyed for lack of knowledge."

I told one young man who had been struggling with drugs, "When you come to church on Thursday night, I want you to get on your knees and call upon Jesus through the whole service." I knew that he needed a life-changing encounter with the living God, not a mere religious experience in a religious setting. This young man proceeded to call upon the name of the Lord, and God's spirit literally permeated the atmosphere. He felt the presence and power of God in him and shouted with the expression of praise in his heart. He experienced the beginning of a genuine relationship with God.

The relationship of sheep to the Great Shepherd is hindered by the twin sins of *familiarity* and *negativity*. This two-headed cancer has destroyed the faith of many who became too familiar with what is holy. We tend to become too familiar with God and holy things with the passage of time. We begin to take things for granted and don't bother to pray, read the Scriptures or spend time in His presence. The predictable result is that our hearts become filled with doubt instead of with faith.

It is Difficult to Lead the "Un-restored"

Our Shepherd's goal is to "lead us in the paths of righteousness for His name's sake."[11] The problem is that it is difficult to lead those who have not been restored because they do not recognize or listen to His voice. When you walk in the path of righteousness, you won't bring shame to His name. You become an emissary and example of who God is.

Millions of saints over the centuries have turned to the fourth verse of the Twenty-third Psalm for refuge and encouragement, and for good reason. David, the psalmist, was a man who faced death continuously for much of his life. He said of his Shepherd: "Yea, though I walk through the valley of the shadow of death, I will fear no evil; for You are with me; Your rod and Your staff, they comfort me."[12]

You don't have to fear death when you walk with the Chief Shepherd who is "the way, the truth, and the life."[13] He has triumphed over death, hell and the grave. Death is but a shadow we pass through en route to the Master's arms. Because He lives, we can declare with David, "I will fear no evil."

Countless times I've received calls to minister to dying saints and their families. It never feels good to lose a brother or sister in the Lord, but God is always faithful in those moments. Much of the time I am hurting because I don't want to see them go. I pray the prayer of faith according to the Word, but at times the Holy Spirit will whisper to my heart, "She will be gone by morning." I just have to kiss them on the forehead and say, "Mamma, it's going to be all right in the morning. When you wake up from this, you're going to see the smiling face of Jesus."

Walking Through Death's Shadow in His Footsteps

Death is ultimately a victory for the saints, so even though we walk through the valley of the shadow of death, we don't have to fight or fear death. We simply walk through its shadow in the footsteps of our Risen Savior, because He is with us forever.

The Lord is still our Shepherd; therefore His "rod and staff" still comfort us. The psalmist used this phrase to describe the two parts and functions of a shepherd's staff in his day. To this day, it symbolizes the authority of the Church and its shepherd-leaders.

The Chief Shepherd uses the end of His shepherd's staff to correct the sheep so they won't wander into danger or meet destruction because of disobedience. The end of the staff is called a "rod." Good shepherds know that correction is a necessary part of their calling. There is no real comfort without correction.

I correct my children because I love them. They may look at me with those big, brown eyes, and yes, something goes through me when I see the tears begin to fill their eyes. Sometimes I can barely stand it. Nevertheless, I have to put my emotions aside and correct them for their own good. As a good father and under-shepherd in my home, I want my children to have a prosperous future.

Any church or ministry that has no mechanism or stomach for godly correction is a "bastard church" that really has no spiritual father or mother. We serve a God of order and authority. Every church and every believer must have a "covering." For reasons known only to God, He chose to use human beings as His instruments of leadership and corrections, and He leaves us no choice in the matter.

The Shepherd's Staff Draws Us Closer

What about the shepherd's staff? The staff is the crooked or curved end of the rod, and the Good Shepherd uses it to "draw sheep unto Himself." It is His staff that lifts us from the cleft of the rock and comforts us in times of distress and danger. No one can comfort us like Jesus, the great Shepherd of the sheep.

God ordained us for greatness and marked our lives for possibility, promise and divine potential. The author of the Twenty-third Psalm also said:

> *For by You I can run against a troop; by my God I can leap over a wall. As for God, His way is perfect; the word of the LORD is proven; He is a shield to all who trust in Him. (2 Sam. 22:30–31)*

None of us can "run against a troop" or "leap over a wall" if we are weak and weary. Yet, God has called us to assault the gates of hell and overcome the enemy in His name. Now is the time to step into line and obey God's Word.

We *must* take time to lie down in God's green pastures beside the still waters of His presence. Take a mandatory rest in the protection of His rod and staff so the Holy Spirit can pour healing oil into your wounds, refresh your spirit and renew your heart and mind.

We have a world to conquer in Christ's name and we are destined to win as long as we remember the Lord is *still* our Shepherd!

— Endnotes

1. Lam. 3:22.

2. Ps. 23:4.

3. 1 Peter 5:1–4.

4. Matt. 6:33.

5. Ps. 31:15.

6. I developed my definition for **hora** and **aion** with assistance from the keen insights of two scholars: W. E. Vine, *Vine's Expository Dictionary of Old and New Testament Words,* vol. 4 (Old Tappan, NJ: Fleming H. Revell Company, 1981), 137–38; and James Strong, *Strong's Exhaustive Concordance of the Bible* (Peabody, MA: Hendrickson Publishers, n.d.); (Greek, #165).

7. My definitions for **kairos** and **chronos** were adapted and expanded from definitions cited in *Vine's Expository Dictionary,* vol. 4, pp. 137–38; and *Strong's Exhaustive Concordance of the Bible* (Greek, #2540, #5550).

8. Prov. 13:20.

9. Ps. 118:24.

10. Phil. 4:13.

11. Ps. 23:3b.

12. Ps. 23:4.

13. John 14:6.

12

It's Your Choice to Act

Whether you like it or not, you make a major choice every morning when you wake up. God has given you everything you need to live in victory, but each day *you* choose whether to live as a victor or a victim.[1] You can go through life as a winner or a loser—the choice is yours. All it takes to win (by God's definition) is the will and determination to stand upon God's promises.[2] It takes courage to draw a line in the sand and take a bold stand for God.

The word *"fight"* isn't as politically correct in our society as it once was, but it is a biblical word and it is a reality in the Christian life. Every blood-washed Christian is called and predestined to *resist* or *fight* Satan and the kingdom of darkness. We are anointed and appointed to snatch the lost and dying from the very flames of hell. Somehow this picture doesn't match the Sunday morning scene of the slumbering saints seeking comfort in their padded pews.

One of the greatest fighters in the New Testament counseled a young pastor/disciple to "*fight the good fight of faith,* lay hold on eternal life, to which you were also called and have confessed the good confession in the presence of many witnesses."[3] Paul the apostle wrote these words to Timothy, and he used eight very proactive "power words" to encourage this young leader in the faith and in the pastoral ministry in First Timothy 6:11–21. These key words sum up what it means to "fight the good fight of faith" and press through life's pressure points:

1. Flee   5. Keep
2. Pursue (Follow)   6. Command
3. Fight   7. Guard
4. Seize (Lay Hold)   8. Avoid

Contrary to what some have thought and taught, Christ did not call us to passivity and weakness. Our faith must be active and courageous so we can live holy in an increasingly unholy era. It is time to act now, because enough is enough.

Flee

The first "power word" Paul delivered to Timothy described the biblical reaction to the temptation and seductive powers of great wealth and youthful lust. He wrote, "But you, O man of God, *flee* these things. . . ."[4]

Peter lived and walked with Jesus for three years, and when

Jesus prophesied that Peter would deny Him three times before sunrise, Peter proudly claimed he would never deny the Lord. But in the end, he failed because he "warmed himself by the wrong fire." He was afraid of rejection and persecution by people, and he did exactly what Jesus said he would do.

The problem was that Peter "knew" Jesus, but he had not really experienced an oxidizing, cleansing, transforming conversion. Once that happened, the same man who failed to stand for Christ in front of a maid stood up before thousands on the day of Pentecost and boldly preached the first evangelistic sermon in history.

We need more than a "church kind of faith." God isn't looking for a "Baptist kind of faith" or a "Pentecostal kind of faith"; He expects to see proof of our "Bible kind of faith." After all, don't we understand that when we are saved, we become *Christians* washed in the blood of the same Lord and Savior?

Pursue (Follow)

Paul told Timothy, "Pursue righteousness, godliness, faith, love, patience, gentleness."[5] Peter ultimately succeeded because he *pursued* or *followed* Jesus, even after he failed. He followed Jesus and walked on water when everyone else was still shivering in the boat and talking about ghosts. Peter followed Jesus right into the high priest's private home the night He was arrested. Yes, he denied the Lord there, but at least he followed the Lord as far as his own strength could carry him.

Finally, history tells us that Peter followed Jesus to the cross and gave his life for the sake of Christ. According to church tradition, Peter didn't feel worthy to be crucified in the same way as his Lord, so he asked his executioners to crucify him upside down. He was a follower of Christ.

Many of us in the Church feel so comfortable that we limit our activity to sitting on the side of the road of life just waiting to go to heaven. If blind Bartimaeus had done the same thing, he would have died blind without ever seeing the salvation of God.[6] His name meant "son of pollution," and he seemed doomed to follow in the footsteps of his outcast father, Timaeus (pollution).[7]

Since Bartimaeus was born blind, he had to scratch out a living by begging outside the gate of Jericho. When he heard a crowd coming up the road and learned they were following Jesus, he refused to sit quietly by the side of the road beside his beggar's bowl. Instead, he shouted and cried out for Jesus so loudly that even the Lord's disciples tried to shut him up!

Bartimaeus refused to be quiet until Jesus turned aside in answer to his faith and hunger for wholeness. He pursued Jesus until the Master healed his eyes so he could literally see the Son of God. Because of his persistence and his faith, Bartimaeus's name was forever etched in the annals of God's glory. Salvation is a freely given gift from God, but we have to ask Him for salvation and all of His other gifts.

Fight!

Paul also told his young disciple, "Fight the good fight of faith. . . ."[8] Do you feel like everything in your life is "going to hell in a handbasket" right now? Can you sense the clutching fingers of the enemy tearing at the foundations of your marriage? Are your children sliding down the slippery slope of compromise in step with the world's seductive tunes and immorality? Are your community and church drowning in a flood of lawlessness and politically correct philosophy?

My friend, it is time to *take a stand and fight* for the people you love and the truths you believe in. Just make sure you enter the fight in the strength of a life-transforming relationship with the living God instead of with a sterile, powerless religious tradition.

None of us can afford to play games with our souls or salvation. Don't play with your relationship with God. Eternity is at stake. Your marriage and the destiny of your children may be on the line. *Live the way God has called you to live: Fight for your life!*

"To fight" means "to take part in a physical struggle or a battle, to contend, to struggle against or to gain by struggle."[9] The only way to fight effectively in the spirit realm is to "lay aside every weight, and the sin which so easily ensnares us."[10] In other words, we have to dress for battle. Set your sights on victory and make up your mind that you will fight *and keep on fighting* until you have total victory!

If your children are trapped in a worldly lifestyle or a deadly addiction, don't assume that deliverance will come "in the sweet by and by." Don't approach the problem passively—*pull out every weapon God has given you.* Fight! Anoint your children, your family members and their possessions with oil; bind evil spirits and loose the power of God in their lives in Jesus' mighty name. Plead the blood of Jesus over your children and declare the Word of God over their lives and destinies.

Jesus has already won every battle there is on the cross. That means your children don't have to go through the hell you went through *if* you are willing to "enter the boxing ring" of prevailing prayer on their behalf!

Fight the good fight of faith for your children, your marriage, your sanity, and your home.

Seize (Lay Hold)

Paul the apostle also told Timothy to "lay hold on eternal life, to which you were also called and have confessed the good confession in the presence of many witnesses."[11] Another word for "lay hold" is "seize." This command is anything but passive. And Paul made it clear that this was more than an option. He said Timothy was *called* to do this. Let me assure you that *you* are called to this too!

Keep

One of the most difficult challenges we face day in and day out as Christians is deciding "what to keep and what to lay down." We should ask ourselves what things are important to us and what things we should let go. Paul told Timothy:

> *I urge you in the sight of God who gives life to all things, and before Christ Jesus who witnessed the good confession before Pontius Pilate, that you* keep *this commandment without spot, blameless until our Lord Jesus Christ's appearing. (1 Tim. 6:13–14, emphasis mine)*

Command

One of the fascinating aspects of standard police training is the way recruits are trained to address suspects with "the voice of command." Every recruit, whether male or female, must learn to *command* respect with a voice tone and delivery that communicates the authority represented by the badge of a law enforcement officer.

No police officer can fulfill the duties of the job using only their own resources or personal authority. They perform their duty by drawing on the full powers of the law and the community they serve. The same is true for Christians. Each of us has a measure of authority in the spiritual realm, in the home and in the Church. We can't perform our duties using only our own personal authority and resources. We need the authority vested in the name of Jesus Christ and in the particular office or responsibility given to us by God and the Church.

Paul wrote to the young pastor named Timothy about dealing

wisely with the seduction and influence of great wealth and the wealthy:

> Command *those who are rich in this present age not to be haughty, nor to trust in uncertain riches but in the living God, who gives us richly all things to enjoy. Let them do good, that they be rich in good works, ready to give, willing to share, storing up for themselves a good foundation for the time to come, that they may lay hold on eternal life.* (1 Tim. 6:17–19, emphasis mine)

Now, with the voice of command born of the Spirit and purchased by the blood of the Lamb, you can declare:

> *I come against the spirit of separation, adultery and divorce. I command every unclean spirit dispatched against your family and marriage to stop harassing what is holy and reserved for God alone. In Jesus' name, I command every evil spirit to loose its hold of influence and deception over your children and family members.*

Declare these truths in prayer every day. God can save your children and preserve your marriage, but you need to speak up and command into being those things God promised you in His Word. No, you don't "command God"; you command the forces of the enemy and the resources of this planet.

Guard and Avoid

Paul also gave Timothy two final "power words" in his first pastoral letter: "*Guard* what was committed to your trust, *avoiding* the profane and idle babblings and contradictions of what is falsely called knowledge."[12]

One of the greatest dangers we face today also plagued the saints in Paul's day: the compromise caused by "mixture" and the infiltration of the world into the Church. Paul battled the organized heresy of Gnosticism; we battle something very similar under the general description of "secular humanism." The spirit behind this ancient heresy exalts knowledge and so-called inner enlightenment above the Word of God and salvation through the shed blood of Jesus Christ.

Many Christians claim to have faith, but they have no idea what they really believe. Much of the organized Church is caught up in a mixture of multiple doctrines loosely bound together by a liberal dose of compromise. Millions of church attendees faithfully take their places in church pews with Bibles in hand every Sunday, but they may actually be "half-Christian and half-New Age." God cannot and will not bless "half-wayism."

My Bible says:

> *But now in Christ Jesus you who once were far off have been brought near by the blood of Christ. For He Himself is our peace, who has made both one, and has broken down the middle wall of separation, having abolished in His flesh the enmity, that is, the law of*

commandments contained in ordinances, so as to create in Himself one new man from the two, thus making peace, and that He might reconcile them both to God in one body through the cross, thereby putting to death the enmity. And He came and preached peace to you who were afar off and to those who were near. For through Him we both have access by one Spirit to the Father. (Eph. 2:13–18)

At certain times, the best way to win a fight is to avoid the point of conflict altogether. Recovering alcoholics should make it a lifelong habit of avoiding bars and old drinking buddies if they want to stay sober. Christians who committed adultery before their conversion must learn how to keep their eyes on their spouses while avoiding contact with people who would draw them away from their marriage commitment. (This is closely linked with Paul's command to "flee sexual immorality"[13] and "flee also youthful lusts."[14]) And so on.

It is time for us to stand up and fight against sin and for our faith in Christ Jesus. That means we need to "get the hell out of our lives."

We are called to struggle, fight and overcome every evil work of the enemy. The Lord has given us every tool, weapon and resource that we need to win in this life as well as in the life to come. However, it will never happen with "couch potato" faith or mere "church pew passivity."

The blood of the Lamb and the Word of God, made alive by the living and all-powerful Spirit of God, still have the power to change every life and restore what was lost today. We have the anointing of the Holy Spirit to fight for our faith, our families and for what we know to be true and right. It is time to stand up in the power of the Spirit and press through life's pressure points in Jesus' name.

You have the power to fight for and reclaim your future in Jesus' name. Proclaim it in prayer right now:

In Jesus' name, I reclaim everything the enemy has stolen from me. I renounce every sin, failure and false love from the past, and I lay hold of every good thing my God has given to me.

I strip away every stereotype, association and addiction binding me to the world of darkness, sin and death. I lay every pressing and suffocating situation, circumstance and obstacle at the feet of Jesus, who loves me. I press through every pressure point in His strength, and not my own.

I bind every evil word spoken against me and every pattern of evil that operated in my family in the past. I am free, clean and holy because I have been washed in the blood of Jesus Christ and adopted into the family of God.

In Jesus' name, I set every captive free in my family. Thank you, Lord, for breaking every chain and snapping every yoke of bondage over me and my loved ones. All things are new because of Your unending love for me.

For these things and for so much more, I give You thanks and praise. In Jesus' name I pray. Amen.

— Endnotes

1 2 Pet. 1:3–4.

2 Mark 8:35–37.

3 1 Tim. 6:12, italics mine.

4 1 Tim. 6:11a, italics mine.

5 1 Tim. 6:11b.

6 Mark 10:46–52.

7 James Strong, *Strong's Exhaustive Concordance of the Bible* (Peabody, MA: Hendrickson Publishers, n.d.); **Bartimaeus** and **Timaeus** (Greek, #924; and #5090, #2931 respectively).

8 1 Tim. 6:12.

9 This brief definition is cited in David B. Guralnik, ed., *Webster's New World Dictionary of the American Language: Modern Desk Edition* (New York: World Publishing Company, 1968), p. 177.

10 Heb. 12:1b.

11 1 Tim. 6:12b.

12 1 Tim. 6:20, italics mine.

13 1 Cor. 6:18a.

14 2 Tim. 2:22a.

13

Taking Time for Yourself

Thousands of people call me bishop, pastor and doctor. A select few call me father, husband or close friend. But my Heavenly Father, who calls me son, has taught me that even in the midst of my ministry and service to others, I need time for myself.

"Bishop, doesn't that sound just a little selfish? Maybe it even seems a little 'New Age-y'?" No, my friends. It sounds like Jesus when He described the second of what He called the two greatest commandments:

> *"And you shall love the LORD your God with all your heart, with all your soul, with all your mind, and with all your strength." This is the first commandment. And the second, like it, is this: "You shall love your neighbor as yourself." There is no other commandment greater than these. (Mark 12:30–31, emphasis mine)*

After I buried five of my very close church members in a matter of months, the reality of my humanity struck home with astonishing force. We serve a God of unlimited power. Yet He chooses to do His will using very natural people with embarrassingly limited power.

My unwelcome season of bereavement came on the heels of the 9/11 tragedy—a violent event that deeply affected our churches. Many of our parishioners worked in New York's Twin Towers or had friends and family members who did.

Although God's magnificent care and power carried us all through those tragedies with miraculous grace, I came away from that painful eighteen-month period feeling as if I might *come apart* at the seams if I did not *come away* for a season. With the will of the Lord made clear on the matter, I acted quickly to obey His command to come away. It was no small task to step away from congregations numbering in the thousands and to leave so many pressing issues without my personal attention.

My Disobedience Could Endanger the Healing of Others

Urgent phone calls went out to my key inner circle of leaders, followed by letters of instruction to everyone in positions of upper leadership in the churches. I knew that I wasn't the only one affected by so many sad events, but I also knew that if I failed to obey the Lord's command, then I could endanger *their* ability to rebound from this difficult season and receive healing.

More than anything else, God's people need to see their leaders *lean* upon the Everlasting Arms in times of need. They do *not* need to see leaders who carry their burdens in their own strength or wisdom.

The scriptural principle of a "touchable high priesthood" exemplified by Jesus still applies to every individual in God's Kingdom, and especially to those who feel called to serve and lead God's Flock in the Church or to shine His light in the secular workplace.

Despite our protests to the contrary, you and I do experience temptation, frustration and pain in our lives. We know it and so do the non-Christians around us. We should just admit our humanity and openly lean on His divinity in the midst of our mess. The Bible says:

> *For we have not a high priest which cannot* be touched with the feeling of our infirmities; *but was in all points tempted as we are, yet without sin. Let us therefore come boldly unto the throne of grace, that we may obtain mercy, and find grace to help in time of need. (Heb. 4:15–16, KJV, emphasis mine)*

Jesus Knows the Pain of Sorrow's Touch

The Scriptures are clear: Jesus our High Priest knows full well the pain of sorrow's touch. He understands the emotion of bereavement and the sadness of loss. He personally experienced the frustration and pain produced by the sinful actions of other people.

When He stood before the tomb of Lazarus, the only man called "the friend of Jesus" in the New Testament, Jesus wept openly and without shame. When faced with the coldhearted and calculating schemes of money changers in the House of God, He demonstrated the sheer power of absolutely righteous anger manifested in direct physical action (He lashed their bodies with a scourge made by His own hands).[1]

Jesus also personally experienced the inescapable heartache that comes when your loved ones persistently refuse to turn from their rush to destruction to accept the loving embrace of the Father. Two thousands years ago, He prayed on the Mount of Olives:

> *"O Jerusalem, Jerusalem, the one who kills the prophets and stones those who are sent to her! How often I wanted to gather your children together, as a hen gathers her chicks under her wings, but you were not willing!" (Matt. 23:37)*

Yet, even this perfect High Priest, our Lord and Savior, and the Chief Bishop of our souls, understood the need to take time for Himself—apart from the crowds, the ministry and even from His closest earthly companions.

For too long, my own actions demonstrated a secret belief that perhaps I was somehow exempt from this principle. Now I am applying the truths from the Lord's example in obedience to His command.

Time to Steal Away

When we experience great success in ministry, our first inclination may be to celebrate or plan for the next great evangelistic campaign, convention or missionary endeavor. Not Jesus. After He miraculously fed five thousand hungry followers in the wilderness, He took time to steal away from His fans as well as His critics so He could meet with His Father in private.

> And when He had sent the multitudes away, He went up on the mountain by Himself to pray. Now when evening came, He was alone there. (Matt. 14:23)

Perhaps one of the most remarkable things I've noticed about Jesus is how He handled the anger and schemes of His critics. Anyone who dares to do things for God will face criticism, trouble and even outright anger and hostility from others. Jesus dealt with hostility immediately by *taking time for Himself* to get alone and seek the face of God.

You don't have to be a pastor, evangelist, bishop or Sunday school teacher to encounter trouble. Just living the Christian life can cause your enemies to line up outside your door sometimes. If you want to know how to handle the heat, take a lesson from Jesus:

> But [the scribes and Pharisees] were filled with rage, and discussed with one another what they might do to Jesus. Now it came to pass in

those days that He went out to the mountain to pray, and continued all night in prayer to God. *(Luke 6:11–12, emphasis mine)*

The Master reveals a unique pattern following this strategic season of private prayer that fascinates me. Several things happened after He emerged from His time by Himself, and I could not help but notice them.

Mentoring, Management and Strategy

As a bishop over many churches, ministers and congregation members, and as a pastor and leader in my community, I am deeply interested in the Lord's methods of mentoring, management and Spirit-led strategy in the ministry.

The Bible says He is the author or "pioneer" of our faith, and I am convinced this applies in more ways than one. If Jesus does it, there is a solid likelihood that you and I should be doing it too.

Immediately after Jesus spent a night in prayer, things began to happen. First of all, Jesus *selected and pulled forward His leaders* from the larger crowd of followers: "And when it was day, He called His disciples to Himself; and from them He chose twelve whom He also named apostles."[2]

See Through Conflicting Arguments, Possibilities and Choices

One of the most important things that happens when we pull away from it all to spend time with God and ourselves is that *discernment increases.* It becomes easier to see through conflicting arguments, possibilities and choices and to make decisions. It is easier to pick out or choose key partners or leaders to help you fulfill your call or specific duties. It was after a night of solitude in the Father's presence that Jesus chose the key individuals who, three years later, would inherit His ministry to mankind and become part of the earthly foundation for His spiritual building.

You need to take time for yourself so you can make wise decisions about the people you relate to in your life, for those key people may help carry your divine calling, mandate and vision into the next generation.

Second, Jesus led His disciples and the great multitude to a level place where He ministered in the power of God to them by healing their diseases and ending their torment by casting out unclean spirits. As the Bible says, "The whole multitude sought to touch Him, for power went out from Him and healed them all."[3]

> *Then He lifted up His eyes toward His disciples, and said: "Blessed are you poor, for yours is the kingdom of God. Blessed are you who hunger now, for you shall be filled. Blessed are you who weep now, for you shall laugh. Blessed are you when men hate you, and when they exclude you, and revile you, and cast out your name as evil, for the Son of Man's sake. Rejoice in that day and leap for joy! For indeed your reward is great in heaven, for in like manner their fathers did to the prophets. (Luke 6:20)*

This passage reveals the way Jesus "downloaded" the will of

His Father through prayer in solitude and then ordered everything He did in public according to the secret counsels He had received from the Father in private.

Jesus Was Led by the Spirit, Not Driven by Human Need

Ministry did not drive Jesus to do miraculous acts of healing or kindness. Yes, He was compassionate and loving, but He never allowed the needs of other people to dictate His actions or decisions. Jesus was led by the Spirit and devoted solely to obeying His Father. He limited His ministry to speaking what He heard His Father saying and to doing only what He saw His Father doing. It's true! Jesus said:

> *"I can of Myself do nothing. As I hear, I judge; and My judgment is righteous, because I do not seek My own will but the will of the Father who sent Me. . . ." (John 5:30)*
>
> *"I do nothing of Myself; but as My Father taught Me, I speak these things. . . . I always do those things that please Him" (John 8:28b–29).*
>
> *"For I have not spoken on My own authority; but the Father who sent Me gave Me a command, what I should say and what I should speak." (John 12:49)*

How did Jesus manage to hear, see and do what the Father wanted done? Perhaps you think this is a simplistic question. . . . "Why, Bishop, don't you know Jesus was the Son of God? Of course He would know what His Father wanted."

But is it really that simple? During His journey on earth, Jesus didn't have a special telephone available to Him that isn't available to us—that would be the equivalent of cheating on the Savior exam.

Fully God, Fully Man,
Fully Tempted, Totally Sinless

Jesus Christ limited Himself to using the same tools you and I have at our disposal. Although He was God, He was also fully man, so He experienced the same symptoms of fatigue, sleep deprivation, hunger and thirst as you and I.

The Scriptures show us Jesus was careful to take time for Himself by pulling away from people and outside distractions to rest and pray regularly. He also told His disciples to rest as well.

After Jesus first sent out the twelve disciples to preach and work miracles, they came back to Him with many stories about their adventures in faith. The Scriptures that follow describe the typical scene in most successful ministries today along with Jesus' uncommon answer to the problem:

> *Then the apostles gathered to Jesus and told Him all things, both what they had done and what they had taught. And He said to them,* "Come aside by yourselves to a deserted place and rest a while." *For there were many coming and going, and they did not even have time to eat.* So they departed to a deserted place in the boat by themselves. *(Mark 6:30–31, emphasis mine)*

Away from Human Hustle and Bustle

Whether your crowd consists of kids in the living room, customers in a waiting room or congregants in a large auditorium, you will find on occasion that they will literally follow you into the wilderness. That is when you need to do what Jesus and the disciples did. Find a boat and float your way to a private place, away from the hustle and bustle of human need.

Your first and most important step to take care of yourself is to carefully nurture your relationship with God. This will supernaturally strengthen and increase your capacity to live the abundant life while serving others in Jesus' name. Jesus said that He came to give us the "abundant life," and I believe He meant what He said.[4]

We must do whatever it takes to model Christ's *abundant life* before our "crowd"—at home, in the workplace or in the church congregation. Again, that first step is often a step *away* to be alone with the King.

God has given us a unique inner capacity for carrying and renewing His life in our hearts. It is our spiritual fountain, our "well of God springing up to everlasting life."[5] This bubbling fountain of inner joy, this unending well of life is the secret source of power that gives you the ability to bounce back from hard knocks! The psalmist declared, "In Your presence is fullness of joy,"[6] and Nehemiah the prophet declared to a people in great difficulty, "Do not sorrow, for the *joy of the Lord* is your *strength*!"[7]

Will You Wait Long Enough
to Become Strong Again?

Isaiah the prophet declared to Israel in her darkest hour:

Have you not known? Have you not heard? The everlasting God, the LORD, the Creator of the ends of the earth, neither faints nor is weary. His understanding is unsearchable. He gives power to the weak, and to those who have no might He increases strength. Even the youths shall faint and be weary, and the young men shall utterly fall, but those who wait on the LORD shall renew their strength; they shall mount up with wings like eagles, they shall run and not be weary, they shall walk and not faint. *(Isa. 40:28–31, emphasis mine)*

It should be clear by now that when I say, "I need time to myself," it means God is with me as well. If you find yourself feeling weak, pull away from your everyday routines and hourly agendas to spend some time alone in the presence of the Rock of your Salvation.

Whether you lack the strength to walk, to run or to fly, the solution is still the same. Spend time alone with Him. Wait upon or serve Him in your desperate need, and He will come to you.

One of the least quoted but most intriguing verses in the New Testament says,

Repent therefore and be converted, that your sins may be blotted out, so that times of refreshing may come from the presence of the Lord. *(Acts 3:19, emphasis mine)*

This phrase was part of Peter's evangelistic message to the curious crowd of Jews that gathered after he and John proclaimed healing to the handicapped man at the Gate Beautiful of Jerusalem's temple.

Anytime you pull away from the driving currents of life to seek solace alone in God's presence, make sure you take care of any lingering sins through repentance. Then you will again receive the "times" you need more than any other—those supernatural *times of refreshing* that only come from the presence of the Lord.

— Endnotes

1   John 11:32–44; 2:13–17, respectively.

2   Luke 6:13.

3   Luke 6:19.

4   John 10:10.

5   John 4:14.

6   Ps. 16:11b.

7   Neh. 8:10b, emphasis mine.

14

❧

Finding God's Will in Troubled Times

From the first hour after the Twin Towers of New York's World Trade Center imploded in flames and tragedy, I found myself trying to guide the grieving members of my churches through the pain and sorrow of unspeakable turmoil. While some of the people in the congregation were still waiting for concrete news about loved ones and friends, others had already received news and were trying to wrestle with the grief it spawned in their hearts.

Somehow, I was expected to help these people find God's will in troubled times—even in the midst of my own pain and sorrow.

Peace in the midst of life's storms requires confidence in your direction and in the Captain of your ship.

King David was one of history's greatest champions and most brilliant writers. He penned a timeless masterpiece of God-birthed inspiration and hope in the midst of overwhelming sorrow and uncertainty that we call the Twenty-seventh Psalm. It will serve us well to read it if we are serious about pressing through instead of being pressed down by life's pressures. Realize that this is part of God's prescription for survival and healing:

> *The LORD is my light and my salvation; whom shall I fear? The LORD is the strength of my life; of whom shall I be afraid?*
>
> *When the wicked came against me to eat up my flesh, my enemies and foes, they stumbled and fell.*
>
> *Though an army may encamp against me, my heart shall not fear; though war should rise against me, in this I will be confident.*
>
> *One thing I have desired of the LORD, that will I seek: That I may dwell in the house of the LORD all the days of my life, to behold the beauty of the LORD, and to inquire in His temple.*
>
> For in the time of trouble He shall hide me in His pavilion; in the secret place of His tabernacle He shall hide me; He shall set me high upon a rock.
>
> . . . *When my father and my mother forsake me, then the LORD will take care of me.*
>
> *Teach me your way, O LORD, and lead me in a smooth path, because of my enemies.*
>
> *Do not deliver me to the will of my adversaries; for false witnesses have risen against me, and such as breathe out violence.*
>
> I would have lost heart, unless I had believed that I would see the goodness of the LORD in the land of the living.
>
> *Wait on the LORD; be of good courage, and He shall strengthen your heart; Wait, I say, on the LORD! (Ps. 27:1–5, 10–14, emphasis mine)*

Living Under the Slavery of Fear

When you consider that Americans think of themselves as "the freest people on earth," it sure is strange to see so many of us living under the slavery of fears, phobias and trepidations so much of the time. As if we didn't already have enough to bind us, we seem to work overtime, adding new official names to our endless list of fears and personal phobias.

Most of our fears are minor in nature, but when the all-too-real dangers of random terrorist attacks, of wars overseas, of financial setbacks and corporate downsizing seize the minds of millions of Americans, then even false fears take on mammoth proportions.

Every day since the shock wave of 9/11 shook the foundations of American life, my confession as a believer in Christ and as a shepherd of His sheep has been, "I would have lost heart, unless I had believed. . . ."

The fact is bad things happen in every saint's life—sometimes through sin, sometimes through genetics and sometimes in the process of spiritual war. A whole lot of saints died in the vicious attack on the World Trade Center towers; a lot of folk who prayed the "Prayer of Jabez" met God that day. (And there is no room for ignorant comments such as, "They should have prayed the right prayer.")

Remember: an ENEMY perpetrated those evil deeds. Yet God remained our refuge in the face of it. We don't know what the future holds, but we know that God holds our future. Our job is to be still and know that He is still God.

Put Your Earthly Circumstances in Divine Perspective

It is time to turn the tide on fear by taking hold of God's Word by faith. Discard the deception of the father of lies and take your stand upon the Word of God. Put your earthly circumstances in divine perspective by *believing* what God says about you and His role in directing and preserving your life!

> *Then Jesus said to those Jews who believed Him, "If you abide in my word, you are my disciples indeed. And you shall know the truth, and the truth shall make you free." (John 8:31–32)*

No matter how many towers fall, no matter how many threats the enemies of righteousness and truth issue against us and no matter how many things go wrong in our personal lives, we have a divine promise that will never fail. Jesus said, "Heaven and earth will pass away, but my words will by no means pass away."[1]

Persecution Is Coming . . .

Too many of us live and operate as if God promised we would never have any problems once we received Jesus into our lives. In fact, just the opposite is true. The Bible warns us:

> *But you have carefully followed my doctrine, manner of life, purpose, faith, longsuffering, love, perseverance, persecutions, afflictions, which happened to me at Antioch, at Iconium, at Lystra; what*

persecutions I endured. And out of them all the Lord delivered me. Yes, and ALL *[and that includes you]* who desire to live godly in Christ Jesus will suffer persecution. *But evil men and impostors will grow worse and worse, deceiving and being deceived.* But you must continue in the things which you have learned and been assured of, *knowing from whom you have learned them, and that from childhood you have known the Holy Scriptures, which are able to make you wise for salvation through faith which is in Christ Jesus. (2 Tim. 3:10–15, emphasis and insertion mine)*

What does this have to do with you? How does it relate to your purpose and destiny? You need to know the truth: There are some questions about life we will not be able to answer until we see Him face-to-face. Perhaps there will be a whole line of people waiting to ask Jesus about the suffering endured by innocent people in this life.

Live by What You Know

However, we must live by what we *know,* not by what we do not know in this life. We *know* that Jesus made us some promises we can live by:

I Will Never Leave You

For He Himself has said, "I will never leave you nor forsake you." So we may boldly say: "The LORD is my helper; I will not fear. What can man do to me?" (Heb. 13:5b–6)

You Live Because I Live

> *"If you love Me, keep My commandments. And I will pray the
> Father, and He will give you another Helper, that He may abide with
> you forever; the Spirit of truth, whom the world cannot receive,
> because it neither sees Him nor knows Him; but you know Him, for
> He dwells with you and will be in you.* I will not leave you orphans;
> I will come to you. *A little while longer and the world will see Me
> no more, but you will see Me.* Because I live, you will live also."
> *(John 14:15–19, emphasis mine)*

The problem with finding God's will in troubled times is the
"troubled times" part. It's easy to find the flashlight stored in the
kitchen drawer at noontime on a sunny day. It isn't so easy if a
lightning strike awakens you in your second-floor bedroom, and
you discover your power is out. Suddenly you find yourself navigating staircases, hallways and furniture in darkened rooms
when you are half-asleep and disoriented. Even that is extremely
simple compared to finding God's will when trouble is clouding
your every thought and stirring your emotions to the breaking
point!

Things are even worse if we don't bother to seek God's will
when things are going well. What if you haven't *ever* tried to
tune in to God's voice in your life? What makes you think you
will suddenly acquire divine listening skills in your midnight
hour?

The Bible says the "just shall live by faith." That means God expects us to just keep on walking in spite of our troubles and in the face of danger, disease and terror.

Take a Walk with Me . . . Through Death Valley

Millions of people have turned to the reassuring and gentle Twenty-third Psalm for comfort in times of need over the centuries, but have you noticed that David the psalmist made no promises about an absence of challenges or difficulty in that prayerful declaration? In fact, God's Word does say through the psalmist:

> *Yea, though* I walk through *the valley of the shadow of death,* I will fear no evil; *for you are with me; Your rod and Your staff, they comfort me. You prepare a table before me in the presence of my enemies; You anoint my head with oil; My cup runs over. (Ps. 23:4–5, emphasis mine)*

Peace becomes our constant companion the instant we realize deep in our soul that *God is still God*—even in the midst of hard times! Far too few of us understand this eternal truth because we just keep our eyes on the problems and obstacles oppressing us. Your heart comes under the influence of whatever you look at and focus on the most.

Our Hearing Problem
Has Become a Heart Problem

We listen more to the threats of our enemies, accusers and critics than to the promises and commands of our Redeemer. Our hearing problem has become a heart problem that affects literally every single area of our lives. We hear the painful stories almost daily.

> *We were married for twenty years. . . . Suddenly he doesn't want to "bother" with me anymore. Some young thing is looking more interesting at the moment.*
>
> *After I spent fifteen years on the job, somebody younger came along with what seemed to be a better skill set. I gave that company everything I had, but all those years of service really didn't matter at all.*

In September 2001, the bottom fell out of the American Dream on a scale none of us have seen or could have foreseen in this lifetime. It was a national tragedy of gigantic proportions. Historians say the teenage generation will mark their era by this tragedy, by the consummate evil of the terrible acts of terrorism on 9/11.

This was no Hollywood premiere—*it was real.* Mayhem in the street, blood running everywhere. One man yelled out, "I think this is Armageddon." Thousands of innocent lives were lost within one hour. As a result, even people who didn't want anything to do with God or preachers found themselves packed into houses of worship and bowing their knees to the Almighty God of the universe. We all need to be calmed down, comforted and delivered from our fear and anxiety and consuming anger over such wrong perpetrated against us.

The Bible tells us in the last days, there will be catastrophic, strange things going on, with wars and rumors of wars. This is that time. And because iniquity shall abound, the love of many shall wax cold . . . so we gathered together to calm down. How can I calm down when I have not yet heard from my son? I haven't heard from my wife and daughter. . . .

We cannot be calmed down naturally. This takes supernatural intervention; it takes more than Valium, Zantac or a shot of gin. We need supernatural, Holy Ghost impartation to breathe on us in this hour.

People are saying all around the world, and especially in this nation, "Is there a word from the Lord?" We need a word from the Lord because we are confused. "What meaneth this?" How did this happen? Why does God let bad things happen to good people?

David the psalmist knew what it was like to feel the pangs of despair and to wrestle with agonizing doubts. He was tired of seeing the evil man prosper while good men suffered. Yet it was David who revealed the secrets of victory in Psalm 27. He was saying in essence:

> *Things are worse than they've even been,* but when I came into the sanctuary . . . *then I was able to understand, to get my bearings. When I pressed my way into the house of God, when I realized that I*

could not bow down to my own pleasures this Sunday morning at the mall, at the golf course, at the fashionable stores or in the comfort of my kitchen with my favorite comfort foods . . . this time I had to bow down before the Lord in the sanctuary.

There is a comfort that is beyond natural comfort, a Word that calms in the midst of our confusion.

God is waiting patiently for us to turn toward Him. Jesus told Peter, the unlikely disciple, something that should comfort us, despite its less positive aspects. The Lord boldly stated the unpleasant problem in Peter's life, but He followed it with a divine promise and prophecy about our secure future in Him. He told Peter:

> *Indeed, Satan has asked for you, that he may sift you as wheat.* But I have prayed for you, *that your faith should not fail; and* when you have returned to Me, strengthen your brethren. *(Luke 22:31–32, emphasis mine)*

It is this kind of down-to-earth leadership in times of crisis that steadies the weakest of hearts. And so, peace to you. Stop the panic and rest on the promises you hear. God was personally involved in your soul's formation in your mother's womb, and He is intimately concerned with your moment-by-moment welfare right now.

God is not shocked when you fail or fall short of perfection, but He is unwilling to allow you to *stay* in any place of perpetual failure, sin or imperfection. He is patient, but He is also divinely determined to lift you to a higher plane of abundant and victorious life.

That explains why Paul the apostle spoke of conformation and transformation so strongly to the Church at Rome:

> *And we know that all things work together for good to those who love God, to those who are called according to His purpose.* For whom He foreknew, He also predestined to be conformed to the image of His Son, *that He might be the firstborn among many brethren. Moreover whom He predestined, these He also called; whom He called, these He also justified; and whom He justified, these He also glorified. (Rom. 8:28–30, emphasis mine)*
>
> *I beseech you therefore, brethren, by the mercies of God, that ye present your bodies a living sacrifice, holy, acceptable unto God, which is your reasonable service. And* be not conformed to this world: but be ye transformed by the renewing of your mind, *that ye may prove what is that good, and acceptable, and perfect, will of God. (Rom. 12:1–2, emphasis mine)*

King David knew what it was to suffer, to be wrongly accused and unjustly pursued. When he wrote a psalm, he wrote from the heart and from the rich bed of genuine human experience, spiced with divine intervention and supernatural faith. He described his response when he felt overwhelmed by what he saw, heard and felt:

> *Hear my cry, O God; attend to my prayer. From the end of the earth I will cry to You,* when my heart is overwhelmed; lead me to

the rock that is higher than I. *For You have been a shelter for me, a strong tower from the enemy. I will abide in Your tabernacle forever; I will trust in the shelter of Your wings. Selah. (Ps. 61:1–4, emphasis mine)*

It's Time for a Recall

For most of us, our journey forward "to the Rock that is higher" begins anew with a step backward in time and memory. It is time for a recall in our lives. Once we settle the matter in our hearts and minds that God does not send or orchestrate horror, destruction or devastation on His people, we have to ask, "What is His will in the midst of it all?"

Begin *the process by recalling the joy of your salvation when you first believed.*

Remember *the passionate love you had for Him and for His kingdom.*

Move *past the years of spiritual lethargy, human achievement (no matter how great they may seem) and lukewarm faith to reclaim the fiery faith of your youth in the Kingdom. And*

Recall *the warning of the Lord in the Book of Revelation:*

I know your works, your labor, your patience and that you cannot bear those who are evil. And you have tested those who say they are apostles and are not, and have found them liars; and you have persevered and have patience, and have labored for My name's sake and have not become weary. Nevertheless I have this against you, that you have left your first love. Remember therefore from where you have fallen; repent and do the first works, *or else I will come to you quickly and remove your lampstand from its place—unless you repent.* *(Rev. 2:2–5, emphasis and insertion mine)*

What steps will help us rediscover our first love and reclaim our passion and dedication to Jesus Christ and God's kingdom?

The truth is that we *all* need seasons of renewal and refreshing! Without one exception, each of us needs to come by the Master's still waters so He can restore our souls. Only through obedience to God can we reclaim the sanity of our minds in difficult times.

Recall Them All!

No one is exempt from the perils of life's work in today's world. The Lord is out to initiate a "recall" in your life and help you learn how to walk with Him . . . again!

While I was writing this book, I spoke to a gathering of seven thousand pastors and ministers about *the urgent need for a recall* in their lives as church leaders. The Holy Spirit spoke to us at that particular ministers' conference and said: "Recall them all! Call them back . . ."

- Back to prayer!
- Back to the altar!
- Back to worship!
- Back to praise!

• Back to loving God again just for the sake of loving God!

No matter what level of success we feel we have attained in this life, we all need to be recalled to the God of our weary years and to the God of our silent tears. This is a time for recall!

It is a time to transition away from the busyness of our responsibilities and of blind devotion to what have become our lesser gods of success—of building programs, of climbing the corporate ladder or ascending to the heights of the social scale.

Too many of us are defective and infective, so far removed from our Source that we are now running on fumes and frustration. Yes, it is time for a recall! These are some of the messages I've received from the Lord to help us recall His faithfulness and our passion for Him:

1. **Adjust your priorities.** Jesus was very clear and direct when He said, "Seek first the kingdom of God and His righteousness."[2] We have become greedy, materialistic and overly comfortable with violence and the machismo of war. As a result, we are plagued by local and neighborhood terrorism along with international terrorism. We've been divisive and we have placed everything in front of God.

2. **Address any and all arrogance.** There is a *divine condition* attached to God's promise: "If My people who are called by My name will humble themselves, and pray and seek My face, and turn from their wicked ways, then I will hear from heaven, and will forgive their sin and heal their land."[3] We must address our arrogance both individually and as a

nation. We have become gods unto ourselves and have forgotten our God who is the Rock of Ages. While writing this book, I listened to an aged Billy Graham unashamedly call us, as a nation, back to God once again. We have men and women who call themselves "pastor" when all they have is one member, two chairs and a lightbulb; yet they are as *arrogant* as some of the pastors with six thousand members and multimillion-dollar annual budgets. Arrogance is arrogance, regardless of the size of the person, ministry or nation slipping on that straitjacket of sin.

3. **Admit your sin.** Make sure you allow the Lord to deal with *your* heart before you presume to lead someone else or point your finger at others. When we admit and confess our sin, we release the flood of God's forgiveness purchased on the cross and promised to us in God's Word. "If we say that we have no sin, we deceive ourselves, and the truth is not in us. If we confess our sins, He is faithful and just to forgive us our sins and to cleanse us from all unrighteousness."[4] Transparent confession of sin and genuine repentance will totally deliver you from fear—even if you are a Sunday school teacher, choir member, deacon, elder, pastor or even *bishop!* When you set your eyes on Jesus Christ, you are reminded that there is much more to this life than your material possessions and physical comforts.

4. **Recognize that He is an "anyhow" kind of God.** God is your refuge *anyhow*. If you lose your job, get a bad report from the doctor, get a flat tire on the way to bankruptcy

court or face terroristic threats for standing up for Jesus and
righteousness, He is God anyhow. You belong to an anyhow kind of God. Heaven and earth may pass away, but
your anyhow GOD and His Word will *never* pass away.[5]
The Bible says, "In all these things we are more than conquerors."[6] In other words, "Even this time of darkness and
trouble, too, will be news one day. This, too, will pass
away."

5. **Arise in faith and trust Him.** The very act of placing your
   trust in your Almighty God releases *supernatural peace and
   provision* into your life. The Bible says, "Trust in the LORD
   with all thine heart; and lean not unto thine own understanding. In all thy ways acknowledge him, and he shall
   direct thy paths. Be not wise in thine own eyes: fear the
   LORD, and depart from evil. It shall be health to thy navel,
   and marrow to thy bones."[7]

Your faith may not keep you from crying or preserve you from
encountering trials or persecution, but it will certainly carry you
through them to victory.

No matter how difficult or hopeless life may seem in a dark
season, remember that the only sure foundation in this life is
the Word of God and the God of the Word.

No matter how much trouble comes your way, if you set your
course and make up your mind to find and do God's will in
troubled times, He will walk with you every step of the way.

Recall His faithfulness and love for you, and remember the

reason you are here. First God gave you life. Then He gave *His Son's* life so you could live the *abundant life* and inherit *eternal life.*

You are blessed with a triple blessing from God, and no one on earth or in hell can take that away from you.

Now go and *be* God's blessing to someone else. Show another how to press through life's pressure situations through God's unlimited power and unconditional love. You were born for this.

— Endnotes

1   Mark 13:31.

2   Matt. 6:33.

3   2 Chron. 7:14.

4   1 John 1:8–9.

5   Matt. 24:35.

6   Rom. 8:37.

7   Prov. 3:5–8 KJV.

Praise for Bishop Hilliard's Previous Work

Stop the Funeral!
Reaching a Generation Determined to Kill Itself

"Dr. Hilliard lets the air out of every excuse that would hinder our generation from experiencing powerful resurrection. This book is a manual to the miracle we all need so desperately to see in our lives and the lives of those we love."

—Bishop T. D. Jakes Sr., Senior Pastor,
The Potter's House, Dallas, TX

"As Jesus stopped the funeral procession and restored the son back to the widowed mother, even so, we must use the anointing and the authority that God has given us to stop the onslaught of the enemy to destroy us today."

—Bishop Earl P. Paulk

"Bishop Hilliard's poignant message to the Church—us—to hear Christ's call to minister to a dying generation, is must reading. He reminds us that the power of God's love among people willing to minister is greater than all the forces of evil."

—David Black, President,
Eastern College, Saint Davids, PA

Safe Harbor Begins @ Home:
How to Develop Effective Parenting Skills
That Empower You to Build a Safe and Secure Family

"Bishop Donald Hilliard has struck a nerve in developing the self-esteem of our children. If the world is a storm, and every day uncertain, this book is a lighthouse enabling parents to direct their children to a 'Safe Harbor.'"

—Bishop T. D. Jakes Sr., Senior Pastor,
The Potter's House, Dallas, TX

"This biblically based book about parenting is of crucial importance in these times of dysfunctional families and confusion about child rearing. Donald Hilliard writes out of clearly scholarly knowledge from a wealth of experience in creating one of the most dynamic churches in America."

—Dr. Tony Campolo, Professor of Sociology,
Eastern College, St. Davids, PA

"Bishop Hilliard's ministry is known throughout the country to be life changing. His latest book is a must-read for every church and community leader concerned about the welfare of the family."

—Bishop Charles Blake, West Angeles Church of
God in Christ, Los Angeles, CA

"Bishop Donald Hilliard brings new illumination to the words 'Train up a child in the way he should go,' with his brilliant insight into setting parameters or walls that keep children secure and train them for adulthood."

—Bishop Eddie L. Long, New Birth Missionary
Baptist Church, Lithonia, GA

"Dr. Hilliard is absolutely right when he insists that 'we create a safe harbor at home by making an investment of time in our children.' *Safe Harbor Begins @ Home* is mandatory reading for those who love and advocate for our children. I highly recommend it."

—The Reverend Dr. Joan Parrott, Vice President,
Children's Defense Fund, Washington, D.C.

Somebody Say Yes!
Answers to the Most Pressing Issues of the New Millennium

"Bishop Hilliard speaks passionately and courageously to the deep and often painful aspects of the human condition. This book will bring comfort and hope to those who have been bruised and broken by the reality of our daily struggles."

—Bernard L. Richardson, Ph.D., Dean of the Chapel,
Howard University, Washington, DC

"Donald Hilliard is one of those rare human beings who possesses both sense and soul, fire and focus, charisma and character. You will find all of this in the pages of this book."

—Bishop T. Garrott Benjamin Jr., D.Min., Senior Pastor,
Light of the World Christian Church, Indianapolis, IN

"Methodist by childhood nurture, Baptist by denominational affiliation, Pentecostal by experience, and Holiness by choice, Donald Hilliard Jr. is *not* eclectic in his teaching. He is theologically balanced, appropriately postmodern, passionately practical and profoundly prophetic. *Somebody Say Yes!* is a scrumptious feast for all people."

—Michael J. Christiansen, Ph.D., Director of the
Doctor of Ministry Program, Drew University, Madison, NJ

About the Author

Bishop Donald Hilliard, Jr. is the Senior Pastor of The Cathedral International—The Historic Second Baptist Church in Perth Amboy, NJ. Under his leadership, the church has grown from 125 members to more than 5,000 and has expanded to two other locations, The Cathedral Assembly by the Shore, in Asbury Park, NJ, and The Cathedral Assembly in the Fields, in Plainfield, NJ. The Bishop and The Cathedral have also been successful in other church plants in New Jersey and North Carolina. More than 50 ministries are at work ministering to the unique needs of the multitudes that travel throughout the tri-state area to attend services.

Consecrated a Bishop in 1995, Dr. Hilliard is the Presiding Bishop and Founder of the Covenant Ecumenical Fellowship and Cathedral Assemblies. In this capacity, Bishop Hilliard serves as spiritual advisor and mentor to many Pastors and churches across the United States and as far away as Nigeria, West Africa.

Bishop Hilliard is a graduate of Eastern University, St. David's,

PA (Bachelor of Arts); Princeton Theological Seminary, Princeton, NJ (Master of Divinity); and United Theological Seminary, Dayton, OH (Doctor of Ministry), as a charter Samuel Dewitt Proctor Fellow. He has most recently served as a member of the Oxford University Round Table, Oxford, England, and currently as Group Convener/Mentor to the Donald Hilliard Fellows Doctor of Ministry Program at Drew University School of Theology in Madison, NJ. He is also President and CEO of Joy^3 Music Group and currently serves on the Yale Divinity School National Working Group in New Haven, CT.

His previous books include *Stop the Funeral!* (Albury), *Somebody Say Yes!* (Evergreen), *Safe Harbor Begins @ Home* (Evergreen) and *Faith in the Face of Fear* (Evergreen).

Bishop Hilliard is happily married to Phyllis Thompson Hilliard, minister and writer, and the father of three lovely daughters, Leah, Charisma and Destiny. He is a devoted servant of God.

For more information on Bishop Hilliard and his ministry, or to order previous books, please visit www.donaldhilliard.org.

Grow in Faith

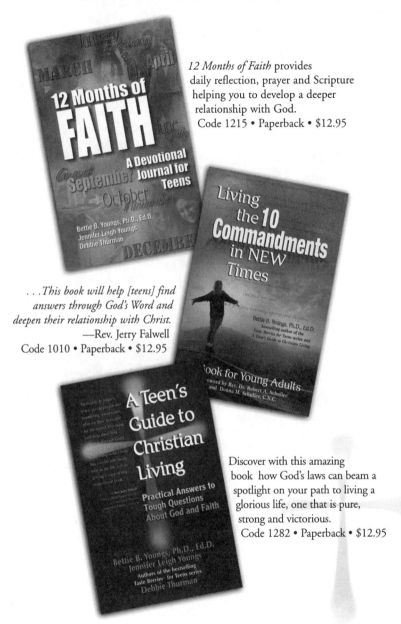

12 Months of Faith provides daily reflection, prayer and Scripture helping you to develop a deeper relationship with God.
Code 1215 • Paperback • $12.95

. . .This book will help [teens] find answers through God's Word and deepen their relationship with Christ.
—Rev. Jerry Falwell
Code 1010 • Paperback • $12.95

Discover with this amazing book how God's laws can beam a spotlight on your path to living a glorious life, one that is pure, strong and victorious.
Code 1282 • Paperback • $12.95

Available wherever books are sold.
To order direct: Telephone (800) 441-5569 • www.hcibooks.com
Prices do not include shipping and handling. Your response code is BKS.

Books from Pat Williams

This fascinating work
will enable you to learn from Jesus' life,
understand his words and build his
traits and character qualities
into your life.

Code 0693 • Paperback • $14.95

Shamgar's story teaches that
one person can make a difference
through God's power. Whatever
challenges you face today, these
three success secrets of Shamgar
can give you the victory.

Code 2203 • Hardcover • $9.95

Available wherever books are sold.
To order direct: Telephone (800) 441-5569 • www.hcibooks.com
Prices do not include shipping and handling. Your response code is BKS.

Books by Julianna Slattery

This indispensable guide shows you how to use your strength in ways that encourage your husbands' potential instead of dominating and destroying it.

Code 2343 • Paperback • $12.95

A refreshing new "blueprint for motherhood" based on the wisdom of Scripture combined with the expertise of a psychologist and mother of three.

Code 2262 • Paperback • $12.95

Available wherever books are sold.
To order direct: Telephone (800) 441-5569 • www.hcibooks.com
Prices do not include shipping and handling. Your response code is BKS.

Rejoice in faith

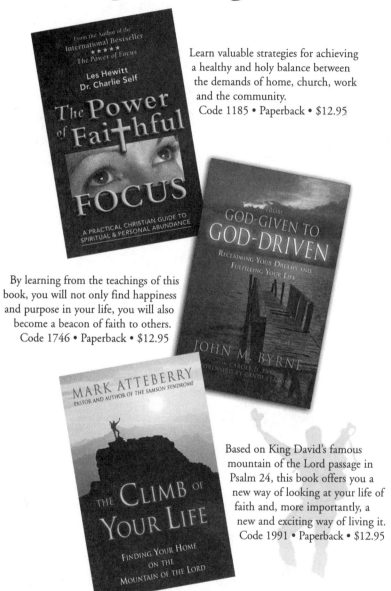

Learn valuable strategies for achieving a healthy and holy balance between the demands of home, church, work and the community.
Code 1185 • Paperback • $12.95

By learning from the teachings of this book, you will not only find happiness and purpose in your life, you will also become a beacon of faith to others.
Code 1746 • Paperback • $12.95

Based on King David's famous mountain of the Lord passage in Psalm 24, this book offers you a new way of looking at your life of faith and, more importantly, a new and exciting way of living it.
Code 1991 • Paperback • $12.95

Available wherever books are sold.
To order direct: Telephone (800) 441-5569 • www.hcibooks.com
Prices do not include shipping and handling. Your response code is BKS.